PHILIP'S

YORK

www.philips-maps.co.uk

First published 2002 as
Philip's Street Atlas York by

Philip's, a division of
Octopus Publishing Group Ltd
www.octopusbooks.co.uk
2–4 Heron Quays, London E14 4JP
An Hachette UK Company
www.hachette.co.uk

First Red Books edition 2010
First impression 2010

ISBN 978-1-84907-077-5

© Philip's 2010

OS Ordnance Survey®

This product includes mapping data licensed
from Ordnance Survey®, with the permission
of the Controller of Her Majesty's Stationery
Office.

© Crown copyright 2010. All rights reserved.
Licence number 100011710

Printed and bound in China by Toppan

Contents

II Key to map symbols

III Key to map pages

IV Route planning

2 Street maps at 2¼ inches to 1 mile

39 Street maps at 4½ inches to 1 mile

64 Street maps at 7 inches to 1 mile

66 Index

Key to map symbols

Roads

Motorway with junction number — (12)

A42 **Primary route** – dual, single carriageway

A42 **A road** – dual, single carriageway

B1289 **B road** – dual, single carriageway

Through-route – dual, single carriageway

Minor road – dual, single carriageway

Rural track, private road or narrow road in urban area

Path, bridleway, byway open to all traffic, road used as a public path

Road under construction

Pedestrianised area

Gate or obstruction to traffic restrictions may not apply at all times or to all vehicles

P P&R **Parking, Park and Ride**

⑩ ⑩ **Speed cameras** – single, multiple

Railways

Railway

Miniature railway

Metro station, private railway station

Emergency services

◆ ◆ **Ambulance station, coastguard station**

◆ ◆ **Fire station, police station**

H ✚ **Hospital, Accident and Emergency entrance to hospital**

General features

✚ PO **Place of worship, Post Office**

i **Information centre** (open all year)

Bus or coach station, shopping centre

Important buildings, schools, colleges, universities and hospitals

 Woods, built-up area

Tumulus FORT **Non-Roman antiquity, Roman antiquity**

Leisure facilities

⋏ **Camping site, caravan site**

▶ ⤬ **Golf course, picnic site**

Boundaries

•••••••• **Postcode boundaries**

——•—— **County and unitary authority boundaries**

Water features

 River Ouse **Tidal water, water name**

Non-tidal water – lake, river, canal or stream

〈 ┃ **Lock, weir**

Enlarged mapping only

Railway or bus station building

Place of interest, parkland

Scales

Green pages: 2¼ inches to 1 mile 1:28160

| 0 | ¼ mile | ½ mile | ¾ mile | 1 mile |
| 0 | 250m | 500m | 750m | 1 km |

Blue pages: 4½ inches to 1 mile 1:14 080
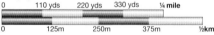
| 0 | 220 yds | ¼ mile | 660 yds | ½ mile |
| 0 | 125m | 250m | 375m | ½ km |

Red pages: 7 inches to 1 mile 1:9051
| 0 | 110 yds | 220 yds | 330 yds | ¼ mile |
| 0 | 125m | 250m | 375m | ½km |

 44 **Adjoining page indicators** The colour of the arrow and the band indicates the scale of the adjoining page (see above)

Abbreviations

Acad	Academy	Mkt	Market
Allot Gdns	Allotments	Meml	Memorial
Cemy	Cemetery	Mon	Monument
C Ctr	Civic Centre	Mus	Museum
CH	Club House	Obsy	Observatory
Coll	College	Pal	Royal Palace
Crem	Crematorium	PH	Public House
Ent	Enterprise	Recn Gd	Recreation Ground
Ex H	Exhibition Hall	Resr	Reservoir
Ind Est	Industrial Estate	Ret Pk	Retail Park
IRB Sta	Inshore Rescue Boat Station	Sch	School
		Sh Ctr	Shopping Centre
Inst	Institute	TH	Town Hall/House
Ct	Law Court	Trad Est	Trading Estate
L Ctr	Leisure Centre	Univ	University
LC	Level Crossing	Wks	Works
Liby	Library	YH	Youth Hostel

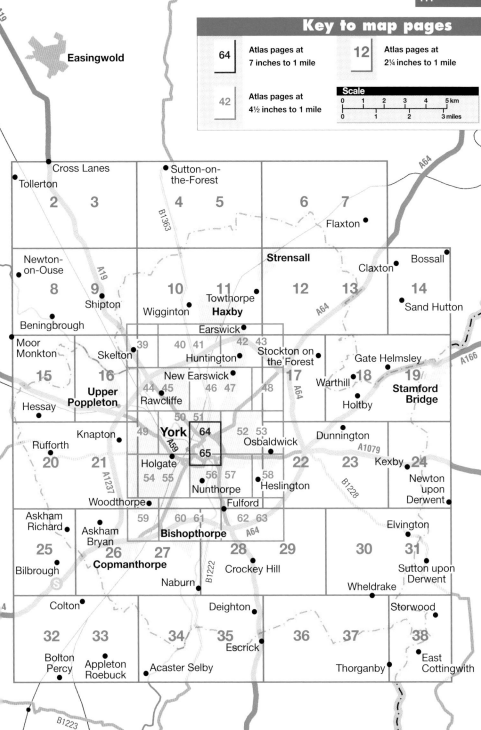

III

Key to map pages

64	Atlas pages at 7 inches to 1 mile
12	Atlas pages at 2¼ inches to 1 mile
42	Atlas pages at 4½ inches to 1 mile

Scale

0 1 2 3 4 5 km
0   1   2   3 miles

Easingwold

A19

A64

Cross Lanes
Tollerton
2   **3**

Sutton-on-the-Forest
4   **5**   **6**   **7**

B1363

Flaxton

Strensall

Newton-on-Ouse
8   **9**
A19
Shipton

Beningbrough

10   **11**
Wigginton   Towthorpe
Haxby

Claxton
12   **13**

Bossall

A64

14
Sand Hutton

Earswick

Moor Monkton
15   **16**
Skelton

39   **40 41**   **42 43**
Huntington

Stockton on the Forest

Gate Helmsley

A166

17
Warthill   **18**   **19**
Stamford Bridge

Upper Poppleton
44 45   **46 47**   **48**
Rawcliffe

New Earswick

A64

Holtby

Hessay

50 51
49   **York**   **52 53**
A59
64
65
Osbaldwick

Dunnington
A1079

Knapton
Rufforth
20   **21**
A1237
Holgate
54 55

56 57
Nunthorpe
58
Heslington

22   **23**
B1228
Kexby **24**

Newton upon Derwent

Woodthorpe

Fulford

Askham Richard
Askham Bryan
59   **60 61**   **62 63**
A64
25   **26**   **27**
Copmanthorpe
Bishopthorpe

Elvington

28   **29**   **30**   **31**
Crockey Hill
B1222
Sutton upon Derwent

Bilbrough
Naburn

Wheldrake

Colton
32   **33**

Deighton
34   **35**   **36**   **37**
Escrick

Storwood
38

4

Bolton Percy
Appleton Roebuck
Acaster Selby

Thorganby

East Cottingwith

B1223

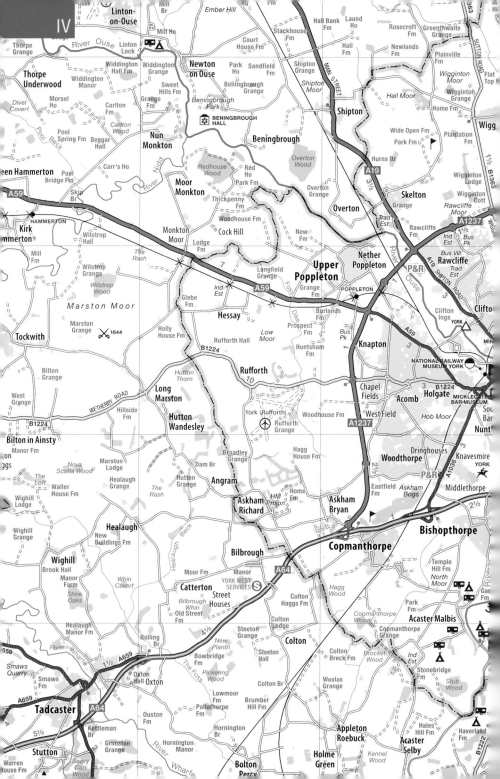

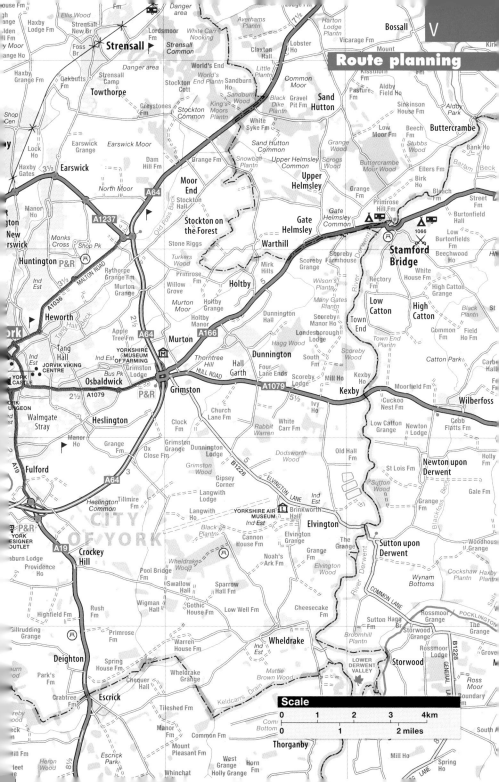

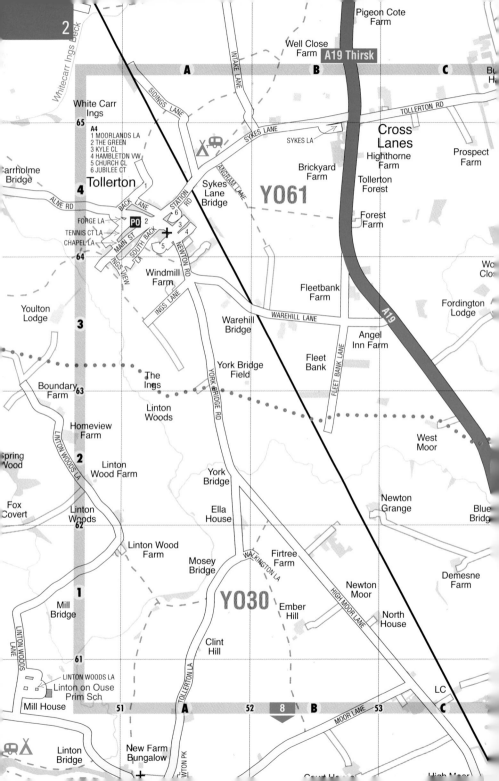

2

Whitecarr Ings Beck

Pigeon Cote Farm

Well Close Farm

A19 Thirsk

A — B — C

Tollerton Rd

White Carr Ings

65

A4
1 MOORLANDS LA
2 THE GREEN
3 KYLE CL
4 HAMBLETON VW
5 CHURCH CL
6 JUBILEE CT

Carrholme Bridge

ALNE RD

Tollerton

4

Sidings Lane

Intake Lane

Sykes Lane

Sykes La

Cross Lanes

Highthorne Farm

Brickyard Farm

Tollerton Forest

Prospect Farm

Angram Lane

Sykes Lane Bridge

Y061

Tollerton Forest

Forest Farm

FORGE LA
TENNIS CT LA
CHAPEL LA

PO

BACK LANE

MAIN ST

SOUTH BACK LA

INGS VIEW

STATION RD

NEWTON RD

64

Windmill Farm

Ings Lane

Youlton Lodge

3

Boundary Farm

63

The Ings

Homeview Farm

Warehill Bridge

Warehill Lane

Fleetbank Farm

Fordington Lodge

A19

York Bridge Field

Fleet Bank

Angel Inn Farm

Fleet Bank Lane

York Bridge Rd

Linton Woods

West Moor

Spring Wood

Fox Covert

Linton Woods La

2

Linton Wood Farm

62

Linton Woods

Homeview Farm

York Bridge

Ella House

Newton Grange

Blue Bridg

1

Mill Bridge

Linton Wood Farm

Mosey Bridge

Walkington La

Firtree Farm

Y030

Ember Hill

Newton Moor

North House

Demesne Farm

High Moor Lane

61

Linton Woods Lane

LINTON WOODS LA

Linton on Ouse Prim Sch

Mill House

Clint Hill

Tollerton La

Wton Pk

LC

51 — A — 52 — 8 — B — Moor Lane — 53 — C

Linton Bridge

New Farm Bungalow

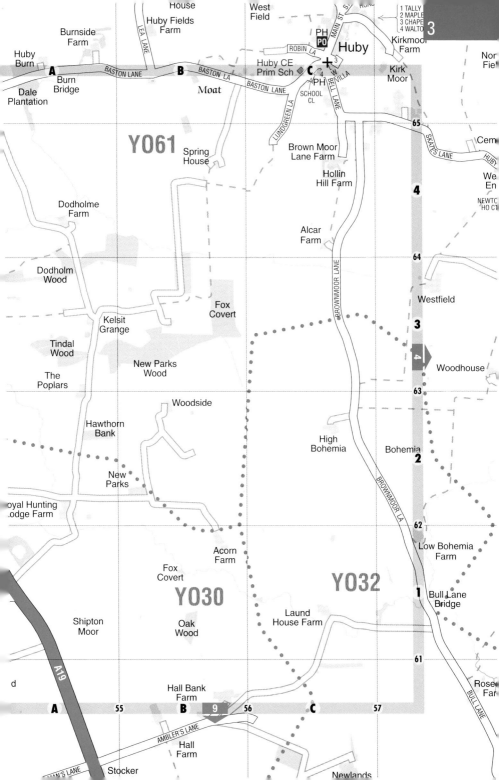

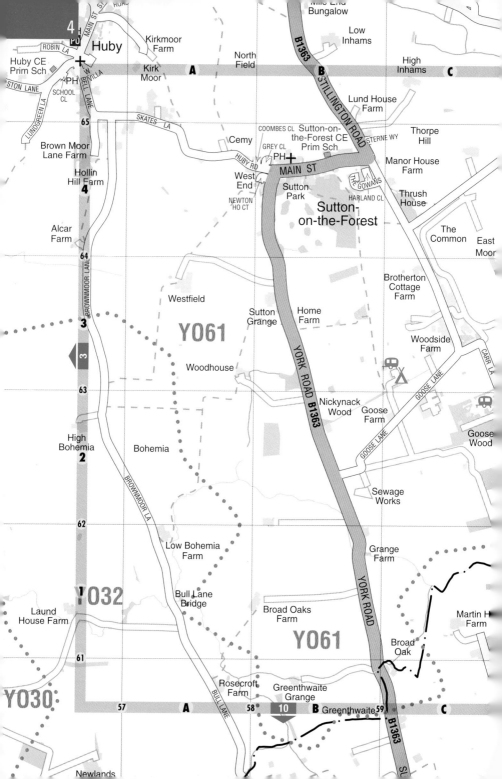

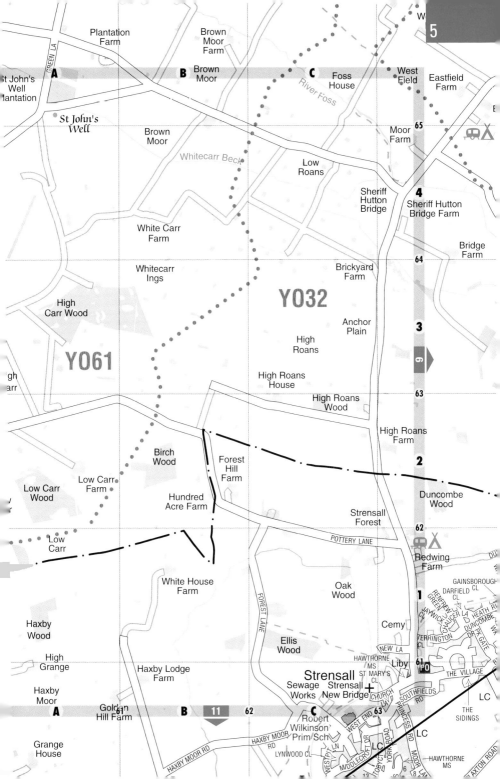

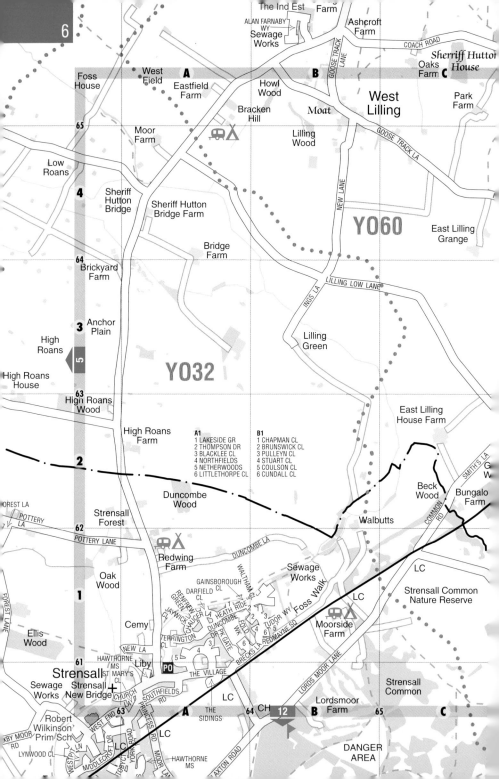

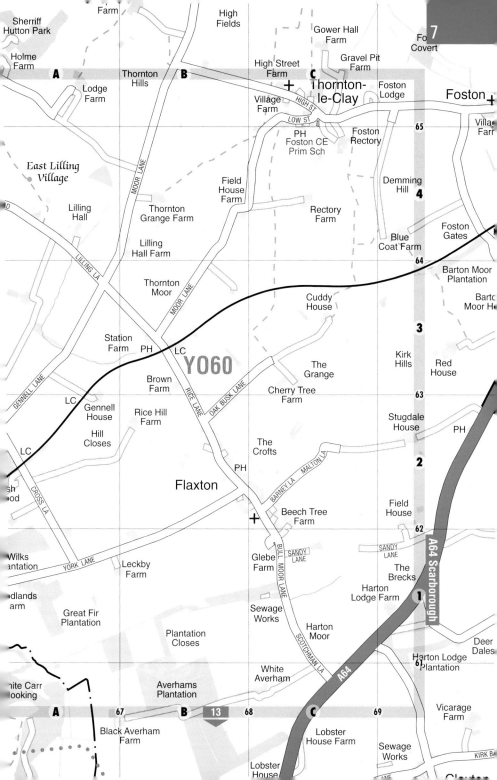

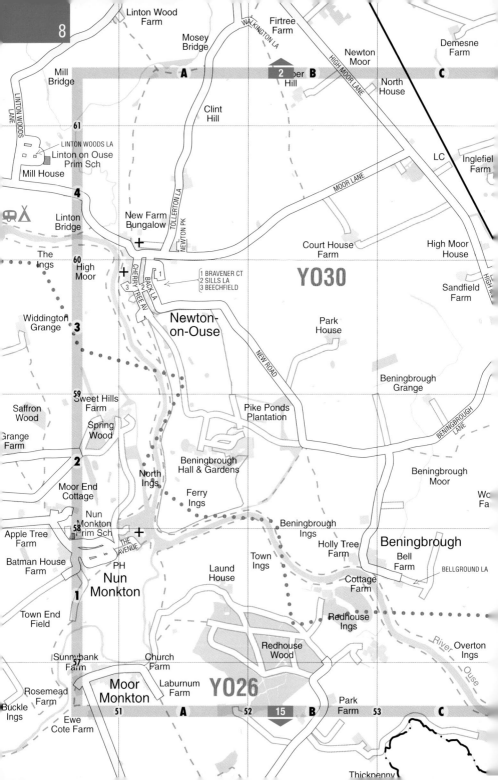

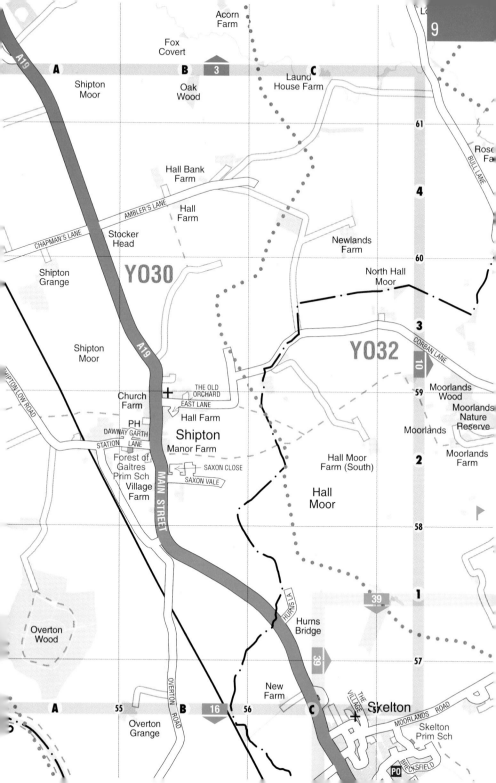

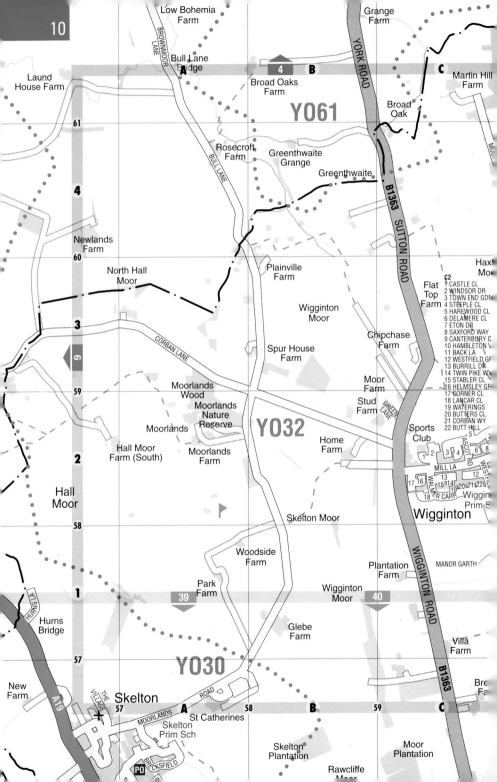

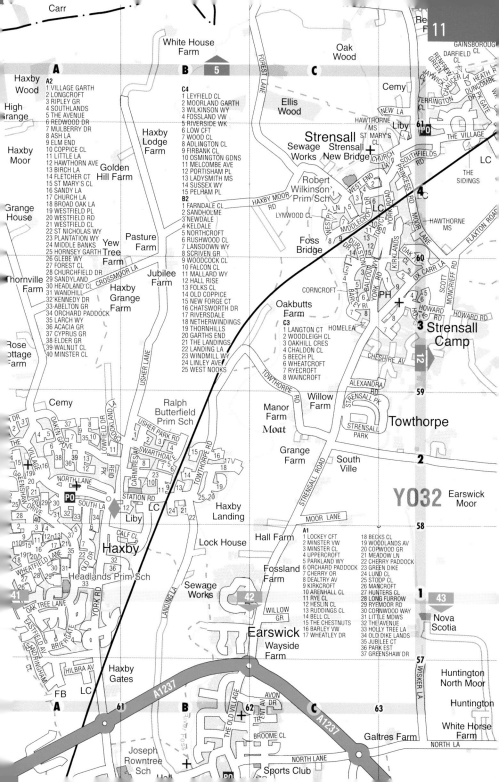

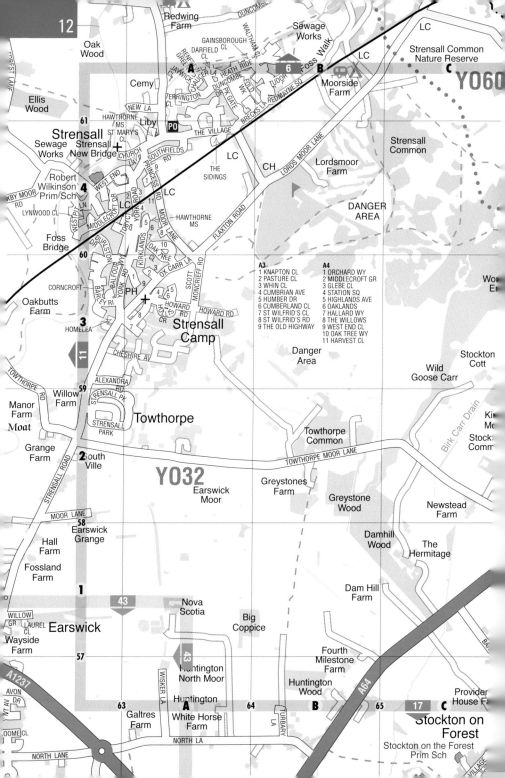

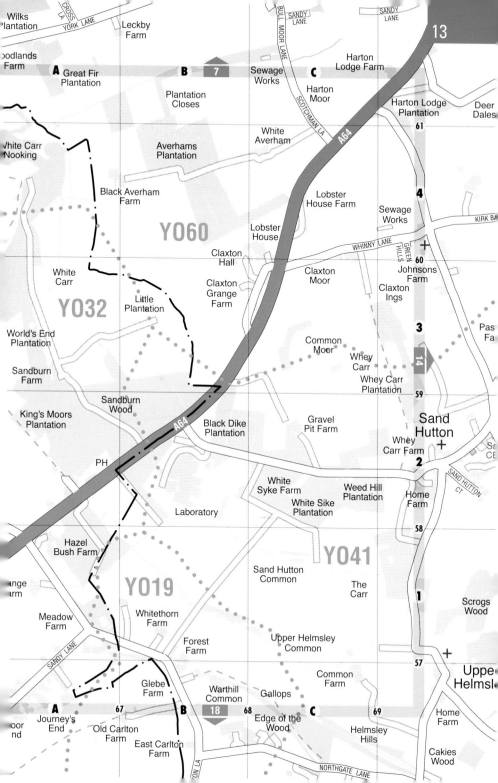

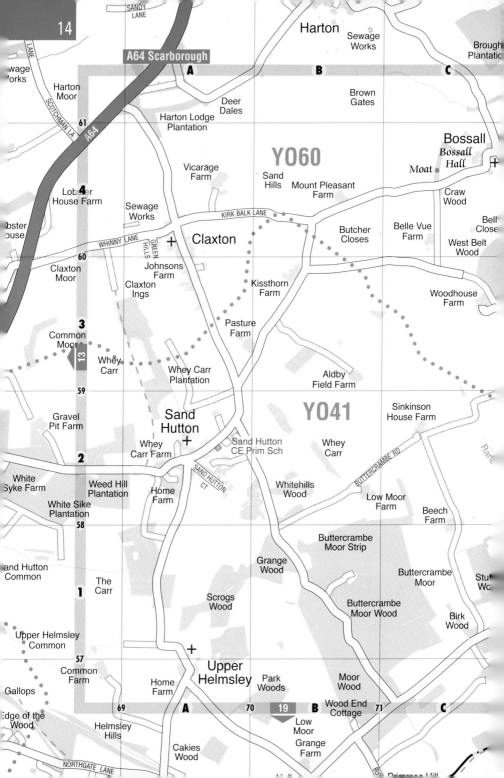

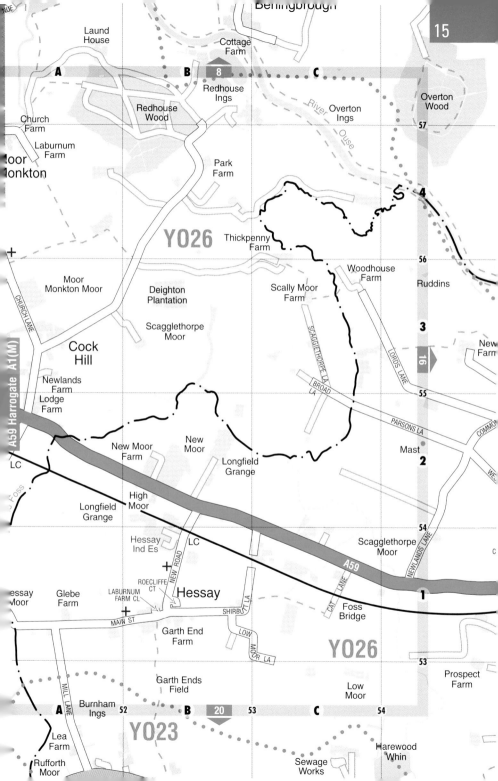

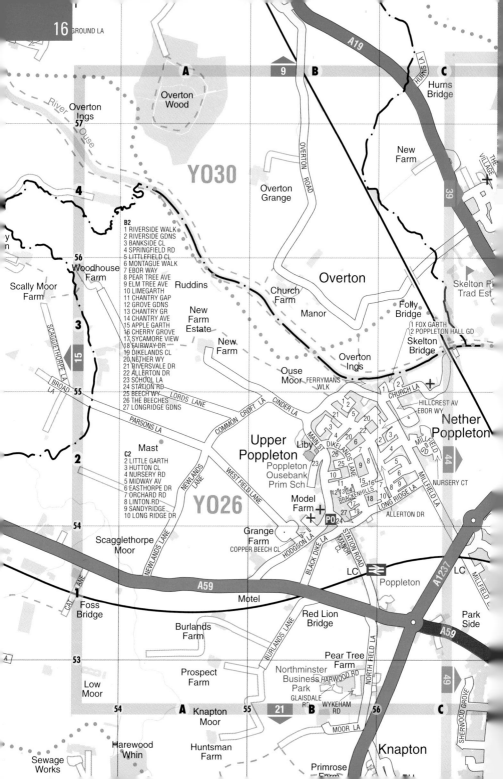

GROUND LA

A   9   B   Hurns   C
Bridge

River Ouse

Overton
Ings
57

Overton
Wood

YO30

New
Farm

THE
VILLAGE

39

4

56

Woodhouse
Farm

Scally Moor
Farm

3

15

SCAGGLETHORPE LA

BROAD LA

55

Ruddins

New Farm
Estate

Overton
Grange

Church
Farm

Manor

Overton

OVERTON ROAD

Overton Ings

Skelton Pl
Trad Est

Folly
Bridge

1 FOX GARTH
2 POPPLETON HALL GD

Skelton
Bridge

B2
1 RIVERSIDE WALK
2 RIVERSIDE GDNS
3 BANKSIDE CL
4 SPRINGFIELD RD
5 LITTLEFIELD CL
6 MONTAGUE WALK
7 EBOR WAY
8 PEAR TREE AVE
9 ELM TREE AVE
10 LIMEGARTH
11 CHANTRY GAP
12 GROVE GDNS
13 CHANTRY GR
14 CHANTRY AVE
15 APPLE GARTH
16 CHERRY GROVE
17 SYCAMORE VIEW
18 FAIRWAY DR
19 DIKELANDS CL
20 NETHER WY
21 RIVERSVALE DR
22 ALLERTON DR
23 SCHOOL LA
24 STATION RD
25 BEECH WY
26 THE BEECHES
27 LONGRIDGE GDNS

New
Farm

Ouse
Moor

Ferrymans
Wlk

FERRYMANS WLK

Church La

CHURCH LA

HILLCREST AV
EBOR WY

Nether
Poppleton

LORDS LANE

PARSONS LA

Mast

C2
2 LITTLE GARTH
3 HUTTON CL
4 NURSERY RD
5 MIDWAY AV
6 EASTHORPE DR
7 ORCHARD RD
8 LINTON RD
9 SANDYRIDGE
10 LONG RIDGE DR

COMMON CROFT LA

CINDER LA

Upper
Poppleton

Liby

Poppleton
Ousebank
Prim Sch

DIKELANDS LANE

MAIN ST

MILLFIELD RD

44

NURSERY CT

BRACKENHILLS

LONG RIDGE LA

MILLFIELD LA

ALLERTON DR

NEWLANDS LANE

WEST FIELD LANE

YO26

Model
Farm

PO

2

54

Scagglethorpe
Moor

Grange
Farm

COPPER BEECH CL

HODGSON LA

BLACK DIKE LA

MANOR RD

STATION ROAD

LC

Poppleton

A1237

LC

MILLFIELD L

A59

CAT LANE

Foss
Bridge

A59

Motel

Red Lion
Bridge

BURLANDS LANE

Park
Side

A59

49

Burlands
Farm

Pear Tree
Farm

NORTH FIELD LA

SHERWOOD GROVE

53

Low
Moor

Prospect
Farm

Northminster
Business
Park

GLAISDALE
RD

HARWOOD RD

WYKEHAM
RD

A

54

A   Knapton   55   21   B   56   C
Moor

Harewood
Whin

Huntsman
Farm

MOOR LA

Knapton

Sewage
Works

Primrose
Farm

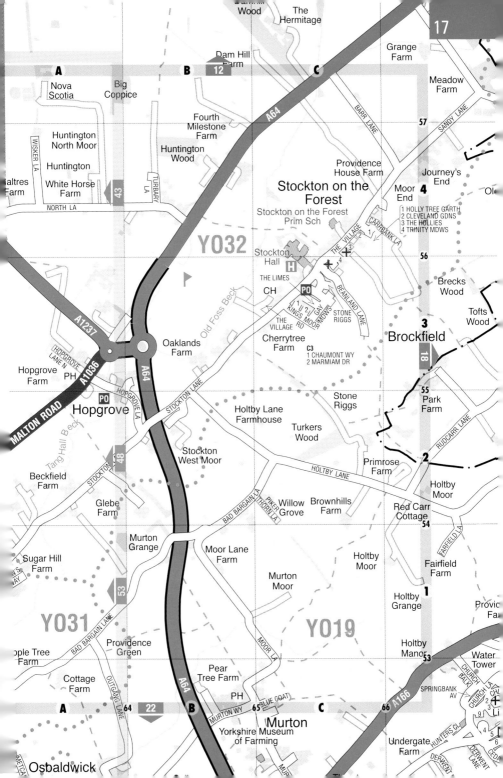

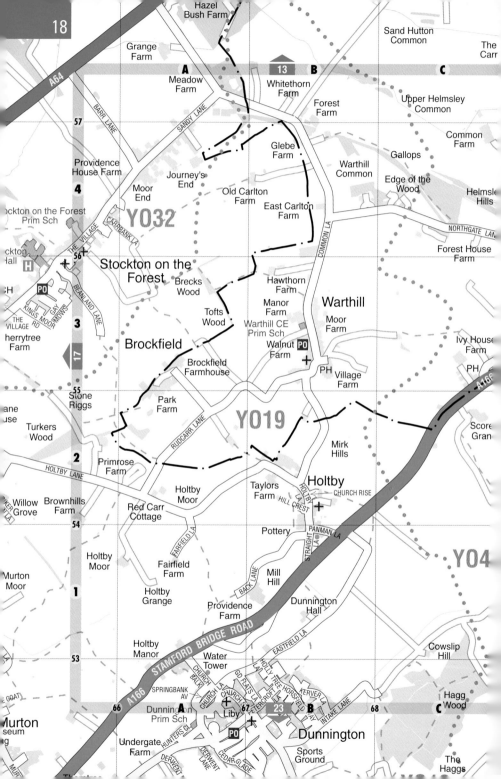

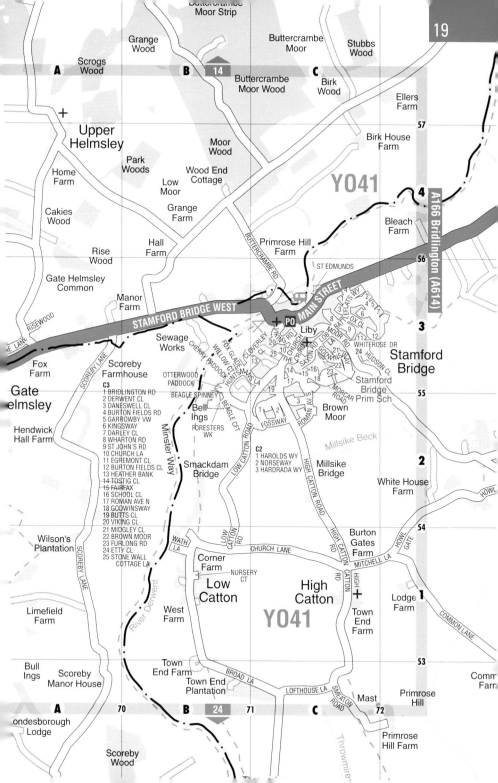

Buttercrambe
Moor Strip

Grange
Wood

Scrogs
Wood

A **B** 14 Buttercrambe
Moor Wood **C**

Buttercrambe
Moor

Stubbs
Wood

Birk
Wood

Ellers
Farm

57

Birk House
Farm

Upper
Helmsley

Moor
Wood

Y041

4

A166 Bridlington (A614)

Home
Farm

Park
Woods

Low
Moor

Wood End
Cottage

Bleach
Farm

Cakies
Wood

Grange
Farm

Primrose Hill
Farm

56

Rise
Wood

Hall
Farm

ST EDMUNDS

Gate Helmsley
Common

Manor
Farm

STAMFORD BRIDGE WEST

MAIN STREET

PO

Liby

3

Stamford
Bridge

RISEWOOD

Fox
Farm

Sewage
Works

CHERRY PADDOCK

WILLOW PADDOCK

FOX GLADE

HUNTSMANS LA

CLOVERLEY

VIKING CL

CHURCH

SAXON RD

THE CIRCUIT

MOOR RD

LOB

GODMANS LA

BATTLEFLATS WY

2/5 ST

OX CL

12

WHITEROSE DR

HUDSON CL

Stamford
Bridge

55

Gate
Helmsley

Scoreby
Farmhouse

OTTERWOOD
PADDOCK

BEAGLE SPINNEY

Bell
Ings

FORESTERS
WK

BEAGLE CFT

LOW CATTON ROAD

BUTTS CL

FOSSWAY

ROMAN AV S

Stamford
Bridge
Prim Sch

MORCAR
ROAD

Brown
Moor

C3
1 BRIDLINGTON RD
2 DERWENT CL
3 DANESWELL CL
4 BURTON FIELDS RD
5 GARROWBY VW
6 KINGSWAY
7 DARLEY CL
8 WHARTON RD
9 ST JOHN'S RD
10 CHURCH LA
11 EGREMONT CL
12 BURTON FIELDS CL
13 HEATHER BANK
14 TOSTIG CL
15 FAIRFAX
16 SCHOOL CL
17 ROMAN AVE N
18 GODWINSWAY
19 BUTTS CL
20 VIKING CL
21 MIDGLEY CL
22 BROWN MOOR
23 FURLONG RD
24 ETTY CL
25 STONE WALL
     COTTAGE LA

Hendwick
Hall Farm

Minster Way

Smackdam
Bridge

Millsike Beck

C2
1 HAROLDS WY
2 NORSEWAY
3 HARDRADA WY

Millsike
Bridge

White House
Farm

2

HOWL

Wilson's
Plantation

SCOREBY LANE

WATH
LA

LOW
CATTON
RD

CHURCH LANE

HIGH CATTON ROAD

HIGH CATTON RD

Burton
Gates
Farm

MITCHELL LA

HOWL
GATE

54

Corner
Farm

NURSERY
CT

Lodge
Farm

1

Limefield
Farm

River Derwent

West
Farm

Low
Catton

High
Catton

Y041

Town
End
Farm

COMMON LANE

Bull
Ings

Scoreby
Manor House

Town
End Farm

Town End
Plantation

BROAD LA

LOFTHOUSE LA

SMEATON ROAD

Mast

Primrose
Hill

53

A 70 **B** 24 71 **C** 72

ondesborough
Lodge

Scoreby
Wood

Primrose
Hill Farm

Comm
Farr

Throwmire

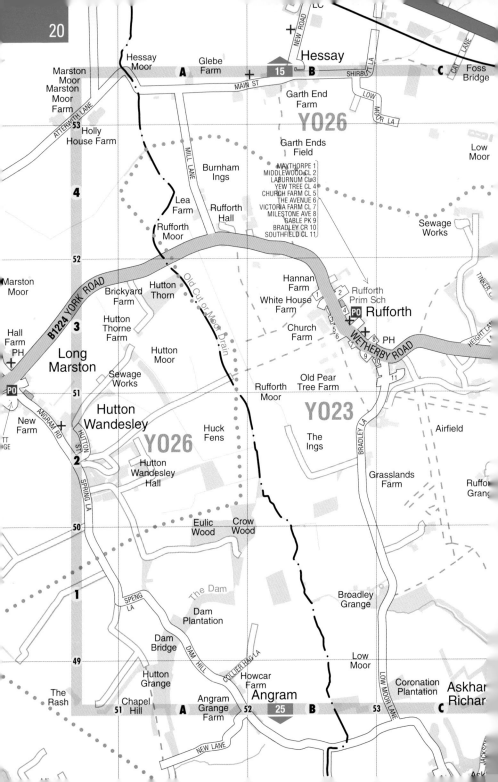

Hessay
Hessay
Moor
Glebe
Farm
A
15
B
C
Foss
Bridge
Marston
Moor
Marston
Moor
Farm
MAIN ST
SHIRBUTT LA
LOW MOOR LA
NEW ROAD
CAT LANE

Garth End
Farm

YO26

Holly
House Farm
ATTERWITH LANE
53
Burnham
Ings
MILL LANE
Garth Ends
Field
Low
Moor

MAYTHORPE 1
MIDDLEWOOD CL 2
LABURNUM CL 3
YEW TREE CL 4
CHURCH FARM CL 5
THE AVENUE 6
VICTORIA FARM CL 7
MILESTONE AVE 8
GABLE PK 9
BRADLEY CR 10
SOUTHFIELD CL 11

4
Lea
Farm
Rufforth
Hall
Sewage
Works

52
Rufforth
Moor
Old Cut or Moor Drain
Hannan
Farm
Rufforth
Prim Sch
PO
Rufforth

Marston
Moor
Brickyard
Farm
Hutton
Thorn
White House
Farm
TINKER L

B1224 YORK ROAD
3
Hutton
Thorne
Farm
Church
Farm
PH
WETHERBY ROAD
HEIGHT LA

Hall
Farm
PH
Long
Marston
Hutton
Moor
Old Pear
Tree Farm

PO
51
Sewage
Works
Rufforth
Moor
YO23
BRADLEY LA

New
Farm
Hutton
Wandesley
HUTTON ST
ANGRAM RD
Huck
Fens
The
Ings
Airfield
Rufforth
Grange

TT
GE
2
YO26
Hutton
Wandesley
Hall
Grasslands
Farm

SPRING LA
50
Eulic
Wood
Crow
Wood

1
SPENG LA
The Dam
Broadley
Grange

Dam
Plantation
DAM HILL
COLLIER HAG LA
LOW MOOR LANE

49
Dam
Bridge
Howcar
Farm
Low
Moor
Coronation
Plantation
Askham
Richar

The
Rash
Hutton
Grange
Chapel
Hill
51
A
Angram
Grange
Farm
52
Angram
25
B
53
C
JACKSON

NEW LANE

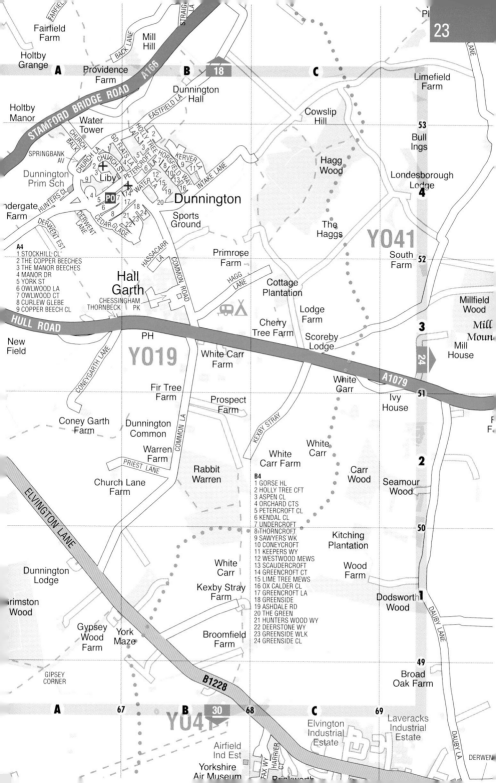

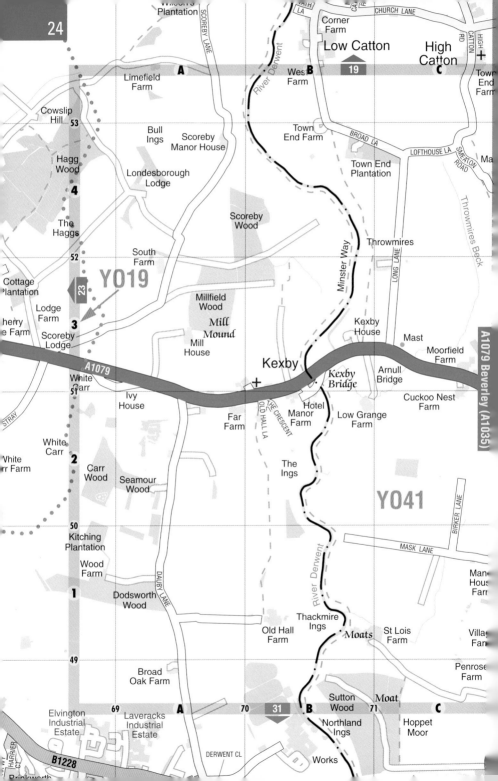

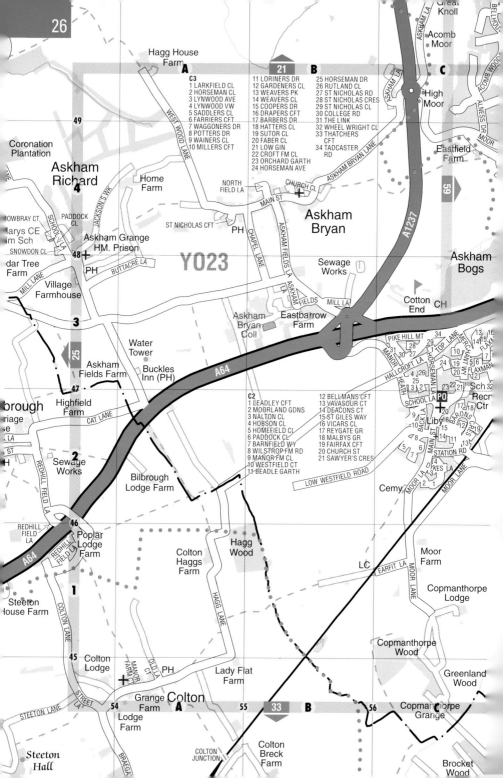

Hagg House Farm

Great Knoll

Acomb Moor

49

C3
1 LARKFIELD CL
2 HORSEMAN CL
3 LYNWOOD AVE
4 LYNWOOD VW
5 SADDLERS CL
6 FARRIERS CFT
7 WAGGONERS DR
8 POTTERS DR
9 WAINERS CL
10 MILLERS CFT

11 LORINERS DR
12 GARDENERS CL
13 WEAVERS PK
14 WEAVERS CL
15 COOPERS DR
16 DRAPERS CFT
17 BARBERS DR
18 HATTERS CL
19 SUTOR CL
20 FABER CL
21 LOW GIN
22 CROFT FM CL
23 ORCHARD GARTH
24 HORSEMAN AVE

25 HORSEMAN DR
26 RUTLAND CL
27 ST NICHOLAS RD
28 ST NICHOLAS CRES
29 ST NICHOLAS CL
30 COLLEGE RD
31 THE LINK
32 WHEEL WRIGHT CL
33 THATCHERS CFT
34 TADCASTER RD

High Moor

Coronation Plantation

Askham Richard

4

Home Farm

Eastfield Farm

NORTH FIELD LA

CHURCH CL

MAIN ST

Askham Bryan

59

A1237

OWBRAY CT

PADDOCK CL

arys CE m Sch

SNOWDON CL

dar Tree Farm

Askham Grange HM. Prison

PH

St NICHOLAS CFT

PH

CHAPEL LANE

ASKHAM FIELDS LA

YO23

Sewage Works

Askham Bogs

48

PH

BUTTACRE LA

MILL LANE

Village Farmhouse

3

ASKHAM FIELDS

MILL LA

Cotton End   CH

25

Water Tower

Buckles Inn (PH)

A64

Askham Bryan Coll

Eastbarrow Farm

PIKE HILL MT

34

MANOR HEATH

HALLCROFT LA

13

MERCHANT'S

FLAXMAN

Askham Fields Farm

47

Highfield Farm

CAT LANE

C2
1 DEADLEY CFT
2 MOORLAND GDNS
3 NALTON CL
4 HOBSON CL
5 HOMEFIELD CL
6 PADDOCK CL
7 BARNFIELD WY
8 WILSTROP FM RD
9 MANOR FM CL
10 WESTFIELD CT
11 BEADLE GARTH

12 BELLMANS CFT
13 VAVASOUR CT
14 DEACONS CT
15 ST GILES WAY
16 VICARS CL
17 REYGATE GR
18 MALBYS GR
19 FAIRFAX CFT
20 CHURCH CT
21 SAWYER'S CRES

SCHOOL LA

BACK LA

PO

Lib

BARONS CRES

STATION RD

Recr Ctr

Sch

brough

2

Sewage Works

REDHILL FIELD LA

Bilbrough Lodge Farm

LOW WESTFIELD ROAD

Cemy

MOOR LA

DYKES LA

MOOR LANE

46

REDHILL FIELD LA

Poplar Lodge Farm

A64

REDHILL FIELD LA

Colton Haggs Farm

Hagg Wood

HAGG LANE

LC

EARFIT LA

MOOR LANE

Moor Farm

Copmanthorpe Lodge

1

Steeton House Farm

COLTON LANE

MANOR FARM LA

OLD LA CL

PH

Lady Flat Farm

Copmanthorpe Wood

45

Colton Lodge

STREET LA

Grange Farm

Colton

Greenland Wood

54

Lodge Farm

STEETON LANE

BRAGGA

Steeton Hall

COLTON JUNCTION

Colton Breck Farm

Copmanthorpe Grange

Brocket Farm

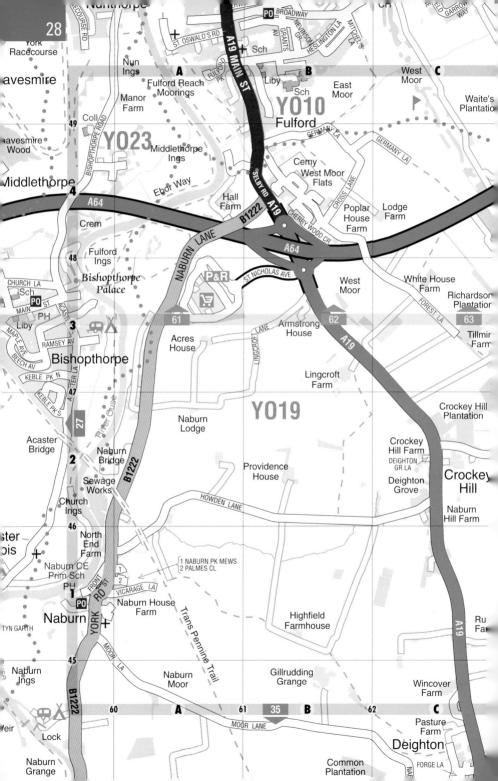

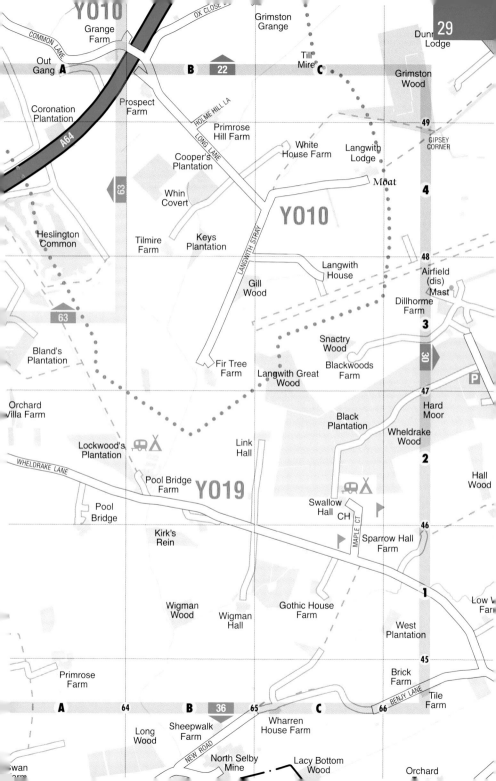

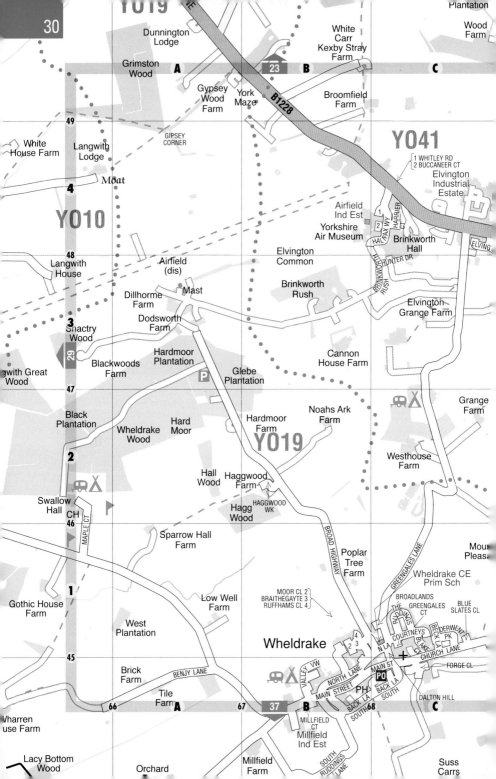

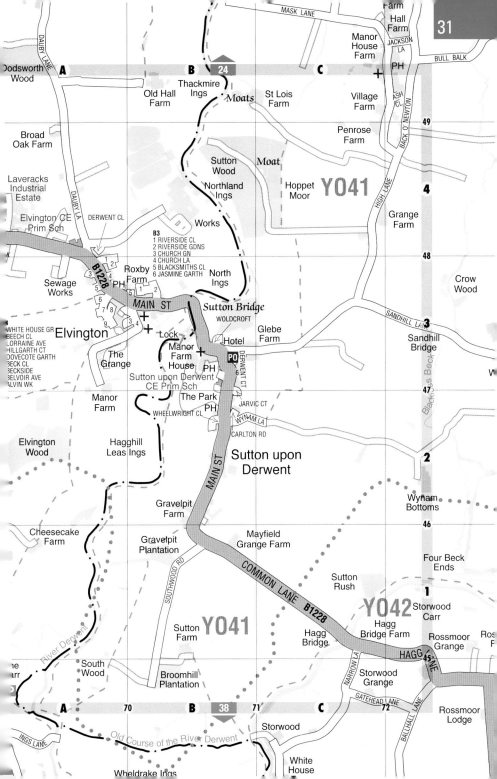

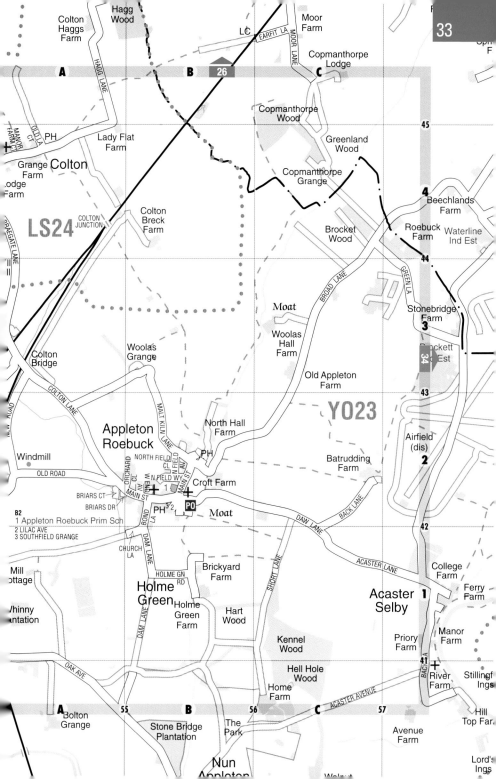

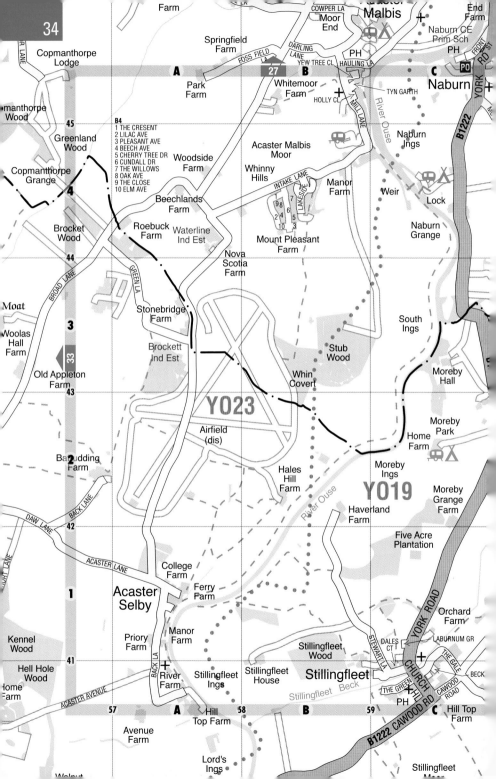

Farm

COWPER LA
Moor
End

End
Farm

Copmanthorpe
Lodge

Springfield
Farm

FOSS FIELD LA

DARLING
LANE

YEW TREE CL

Malbis

Naburn CE
Prim Sch

PH

HAULING LA

PH

Naburn

PO

Park
Farm

27

Whitemoor
Farm

HOLLY CL

TYN GARTH

A MILL LANE

River Ouse

45

Greenland
Wood

Woodside
Farm

Acaster Malbis
Moor

Naburn
Ings

manthorpe
Wood

B4
1 THE CRESENT
2 LILAC AVE
3 PLEASANT AVE
4 BEECH AVE
5 CHERRY TREE DR
6 CUNDALL DR
7 THE WILLOWS
8 OAK AVE
9 THE CLOSE
10 ELM AVE

Whinny
Hills

INTAKE LANE

LAKESIDE

Manor
Farm

Weir

Copmanthorpe
Grange

4

Beechlands
Farm

9 8
2 4
10

7
6
5
3

Lock

Naburn
Grange

Brocket
Wood

Roebuck
Farm

GREEN LA

Waterline
Ind Est

Mount Pleasant
Farm

44

Nova
Scotia
Farm

BROAD LANE

Stonebridge
Farm

South
Ings

Moat

3

Brockett
Ind Est

Stub
Wood

Moreby
Hall

Woolas
Hall
Farm

33

Old Appleton
Farm

43

Whin
Covert

YO23

Home
Farm

Moreby
Park

Ba udding
Farm

2

Airfield
(dis)

Hales
Hill
Farm

Moreby
Ings

YO19

Moreby
Grange
Farm

BACK LANE

42

DAW LANE

ACASTER LANE

College
Farm

River Ouse

Haverland
Farm

Five Acre
Plantation

YORK ROAD

Orchard
Farm

Acaster
Selby

Ferry
Farm

1

Kennel
Wood

Priory
Farm

Manor
Farm

Stillingfleet
Wood

STEWART LA

DALES
CT

LABURNUM GR

Hell Hole
Wood

41

BACK LA

River
Farm

Stillingfleet
Ings

Stillingfleet
House

Stillingfleet

THE GREEN

CHURCH HILL

THE GALE

BECK

Home
Farm

ACASTER AVENUE

Stillingfleet Beck

PH

CAWOOD ROAD

57

A

58

59

C

Hill
Top Farm

B

Avenue
Farm

Hill Top
Farm

B1222 CAWOOD RD

Lord's
Ings

Stillingfleet

Walnut

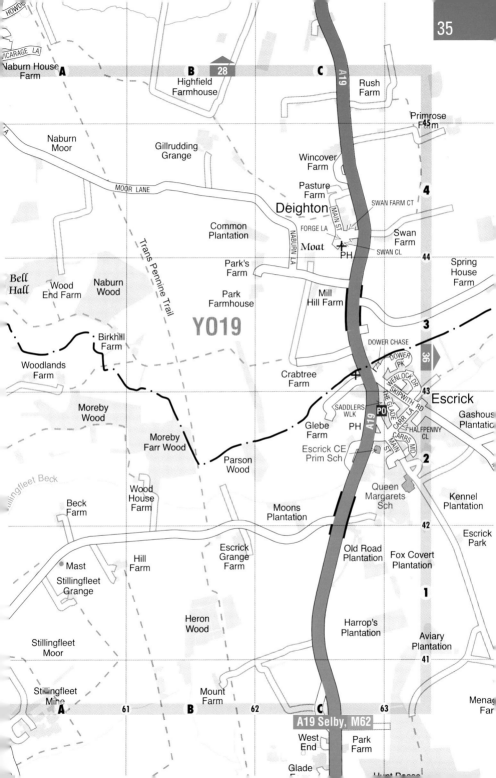

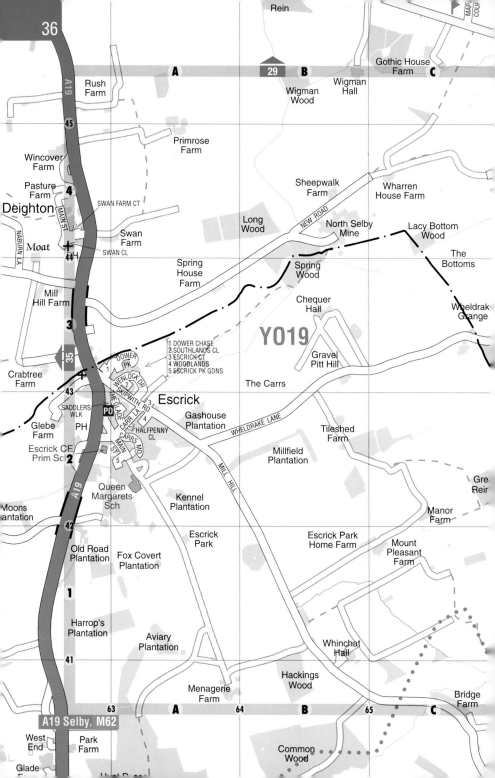

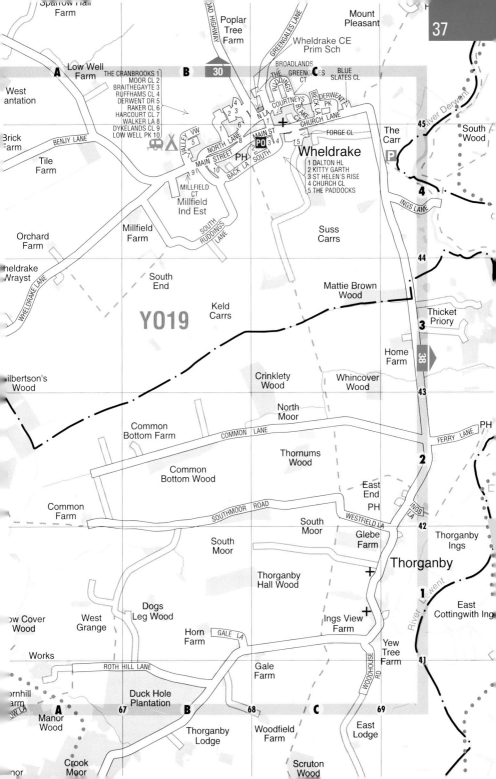

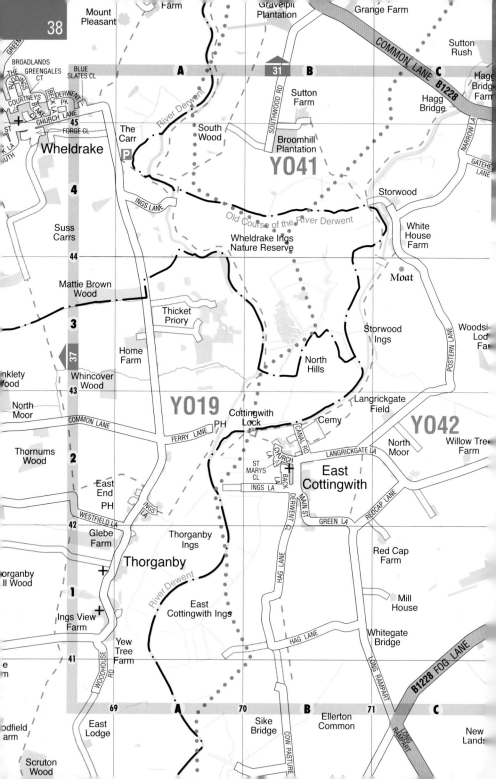

Mount Pleasant

Farm

Gravelpit Plantation

Grange Farm

Sutton Rush

COMMON LANE

B1228

GREEN

BROADLANDS

THE RUDDINGS

COURTNEYS

GREENGALES CT

BLUE SLATES CL

BECK LA

BEDERWENT PK

CHURCH LANE

45

FORGE CL

ST

Wheldrake

A

31

B

C

Hagg Bridge Farm

Southwood Rd

Sutton Farm

South Wood

Hagg Bridge

MARROW LA

GATEHE LANE

The Carr

P

Broomhill Plantation

YO41

4

INGS LANE

Suss Carrs

Storwood

44

Old Course of the River Derwent

White House Farm

Mattie Brown Wood

Wheldrake Ings Nature Reserve

Moat

3

Thicket Priory

Storwood Ings

Woodsi Lod Fa

37

Home Farm

Whincover Wood

North Hills

POSTERN LANE

nklety ood

43

YO19

Langrickgate Field

YO042

North Moor

COMMON LANE

Cottingwith Lock

PH

Cemy

North Moor

Willow Tre Farm

Thornums Wood

FERRY LANE

CANAL RD

Langrickgate la

2

East End PH

WESTFIELD LA

INGS LA

St Marys Cl

BACK LA

CHURCH LA

East Cottingwith

42

Glebe Farm

Thorganby Ings

INGS LA

DERWENT CT

MAIN ST

GREEN LA

REDCAP LANE

organby ll Wood

Thorganby

River Derwent

Red Cap Farm

1

Ings View Farm

East Cottingwith Ings

HAG LANE

Mill House

Whitegate Bridge

41

WOODHOUSE RD

Yew Tree Farm

HAG LANE

LONG RAMPART

B1228 FOG LANE

e m

69

A

70

B

71

C

East Lodge

Sike Bridge

COW PASTURE

Ellerton Common

LONG RAMPART

New Lands

odfield arm

Scruton Wood

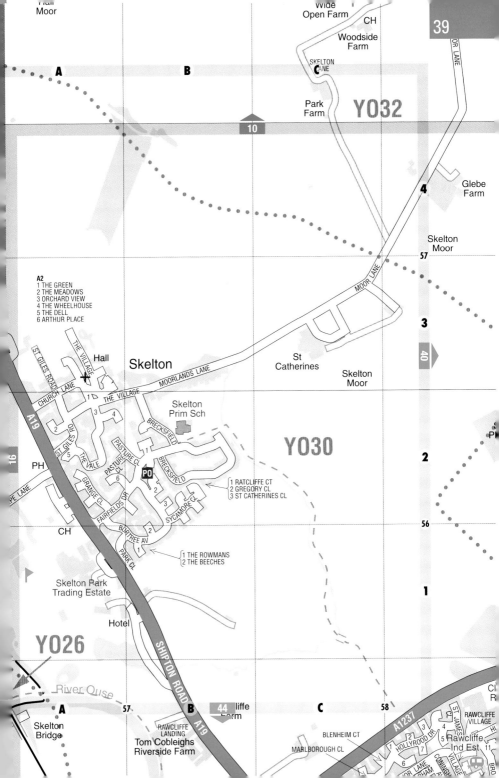

Hall
Moor

Wide
Open Farm   CH

Woodside
Farm

SKELTON
LANE   C

Park
Farm   YO32

Woodside
Farm

39

MOOR LANE

A   B   C   10

4   Glebe
Farm

Skelton
Moor   57

MOOR LANE

A2
1 THE GREEN
2 THE MEADOWS
3 ORCHARD VIEW
4 THE WHEELHOUSE
5 THE DELL
6 ARTHUR PLACE

3

40

ST GILES ROAD

THE VILLAGE

Hall   Skelton

CHURCH LANE   THE VILLAGE   MOORLANDS LANE

St
Catherines

Skelton
Moor

Skelton
Prim Sch

BRECKSFIELD

2

YO30

ST GILES RD

THE VALE   PASTURE CL   BRECKSFIELD

PO

1 RATCLIFFE CT
2 GREGORY CL
3 ST CATHERINES CL

PH   GRANGE CL   FAIRFIELDS DR

SYCAMORE CL

56

CH   BURTREE AV

PE LANE

PARK CL   1 THE ROWMANS
2 THE BEECHES

16   A19

Skelton Park
Trading Estate

1

Hotel

YO26

SHIPTON ROAD   A19

River Ouse

A   57   B   44   liffe
Farm   C   58   A1237

Skelton
Bridge

RAWCLIFFE
LANDING

Tom Cobleighs
Riverside Farm

BLENHEIM CT

MARLBOROUGH CL

HOLLYROOD DR

ST JAMES

RAWCLIFFE
VILLAGE

Rawcliffe
Ind Est   11

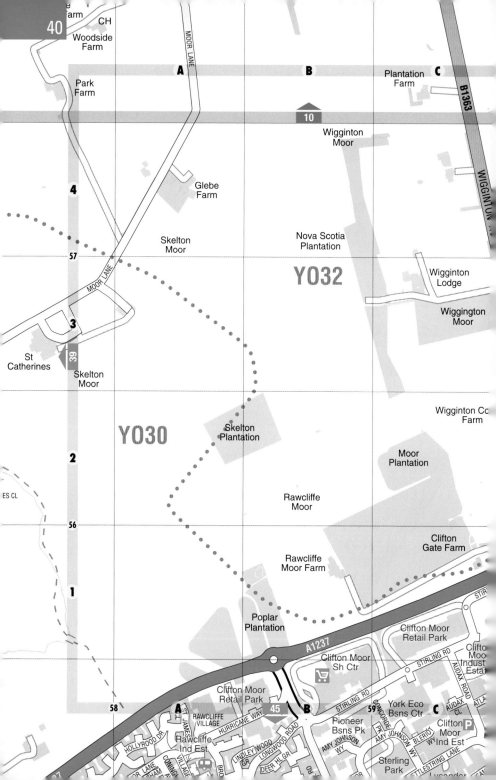

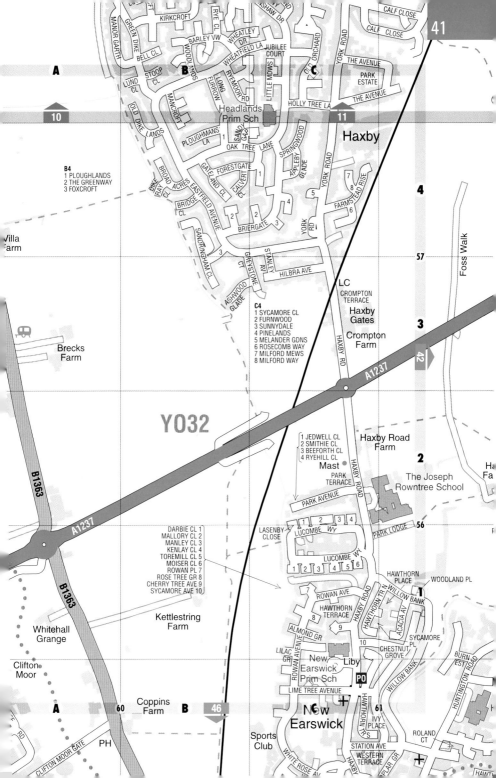

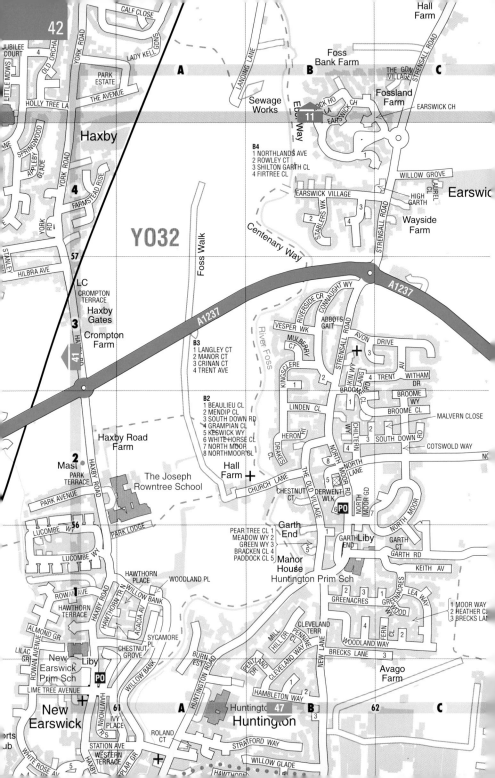

CALF CLOSE
JUBILEE COURT
LITTLE MDWS
OLD ORCHA
YORK ROAD
LADY KELL GDNS
LANDING LANE
Hall Farm
Foss Bank Farm
THE GDN VILLAGE
STRENSALL ROAD
C
PARK ESTATE
THE AVENUE
HOLLY TREE LA
A
B
Sewage Works
Ebor Way
11
ICK HO LA
EARSWICK CH
Fossland Farm
EARSWICK CH
Haxby
SPRINGWOOD GLADE
APPLEBY GLADE
YORK ROAD
4
FARMSTEAD RISE
WILLOW GROVE
LAUREL CL
HIGH GARTH
Earswic

B4
1 NORTHLANDS AVE
2 ROWLEY CT
3 SHILTON GARTH CL
4 FIRTREE CL

EARSWICK VILLAGE
STABLERS WK
3
4
Wayside Farm

YO32

Foss Walk

Centenary Way

River Foss

A1237

A1237

CONNAUGHT WY
RIVERSIDE CR
ABBOTS GAIT
STRENSALL ROAD
AVON DRIVE
3
TRENT AV
WITHAM DR
VESPER WK
MULBERRY
KINGSCLERE
1
IKIN WY
LANG
4
BROOME
BROOME WY
BROOME CL
SOUTH DOWN
MALVERN CLOSE
COTSWOLD WAY
NO

YORK RD
STANLEY
HILBRA AVE
57
LC
CROMPTON TERRACE
Haxby Gates
HAXBY ROAD
41
3
Crompton Farm

B3
1 LANGLEY CT
2 MANOR CT
3 CRINAN CT
4 TRENT AVE

B2
1 BEAULIEU CL
2 MENDIP CL
3 SOUTH DOWN RD
4 GRAMPIAN CL
5 KESWICK WY
6 WHITE HORSE CL
7 NORTH MOOR
8 NORTHMOOR CL

LINDEN CL
HERON RI
DRAKES CL
CHILTERN WY
NORTH LANE
4
3
SOUTH DOWN

Haxby Road Farm

Mast
2
PARK TERRACE
PARK AVENUE

The Joseph Rowntree School

PARK LODGE

Hall Farm
CHURCH LANE
CHESTNUT CT
THE OLD VILLAGE
DERWENT WLK
8
5
6 PO
NORTH MOOR RD
NORTH MOOR GD
NORTH MOOR

LUCOMBE WY
56
LUCOMBE WY

HAWTHORN PLACE
WOODLAND PL
WILLOW BANK

PEAR TREE CL 1
MEADOW WY 2
GREEN WY 3
BRACKEN CL 4
PADDOCK CL 5
Garth End
GARTH END
Liby
GARTH CT
GARTH RD
KEITH AV
1 MOOR WAY
2 HEATHER C
3 BRECKS LA

Manor House
Huntington Prim Sch
GREENACRES
2
3
1
GREENACRES
FERNWOOD
LEA WAY
2

ROWAN AVE
1
HAWTHORN TERRACE
HAXBY ROAD
HAWTHORN TRN
ACACIA AV
SYCAMORE PL
ALMOND GR
CHESTNUT GROVE
WILLOW BANK
BURN ESTATE
HUNTINGTON ROAD
MILL HILL DR
PENTLAND DR
CLEVELAND TERR
PENNINE
CLEVELAND WAY
NEW LANE
WOODLAND WAY
FERN CL
2
BRECKS LANE
3
Avago Farm

LILAC GR
ROWAN AVENUE
New Earswick Prim Sch
Liby
PO
LIME TREE AVENUE
New Earswick
HAXBY RD
61
IVY PLACE
STATION AVE
WESTERN TERRACE
ROLAND CT
POPLAR GR
Huntington
47
A
B
HAMBLETON WAY
1
2
3
Huntington
STRATFORD WAY
WILLOW GLADE
62
C
WHITE ROSE AV
HAWTHORN

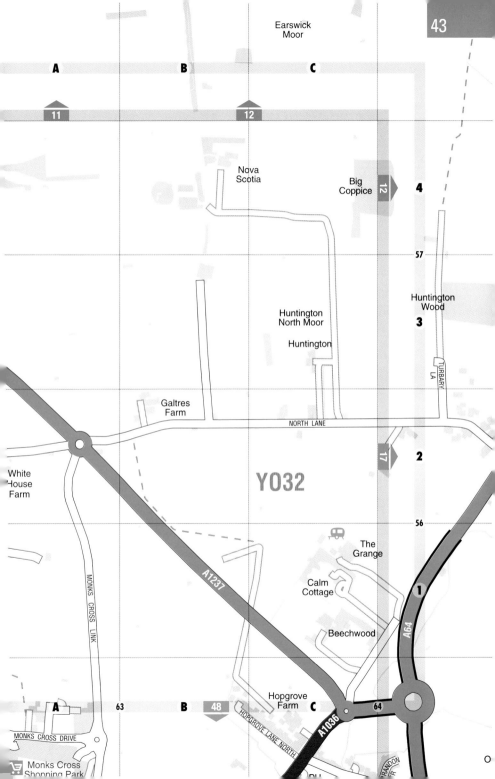

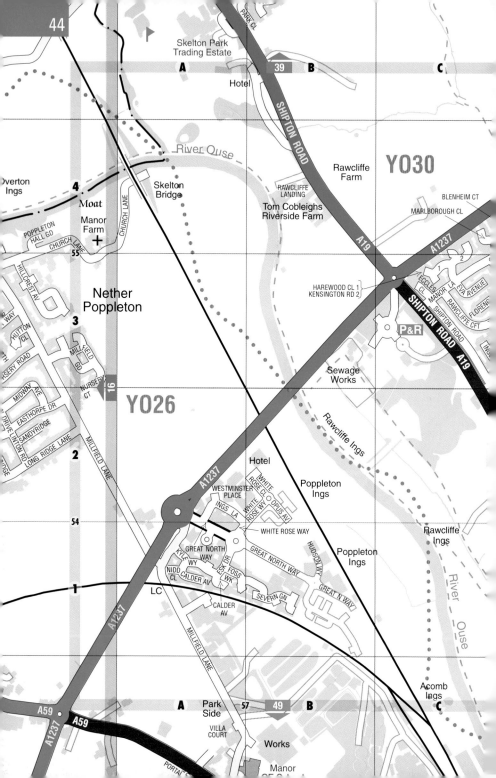

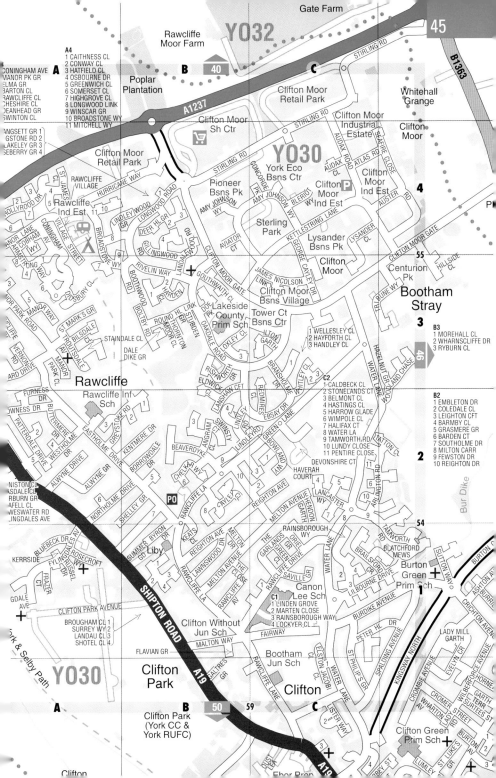

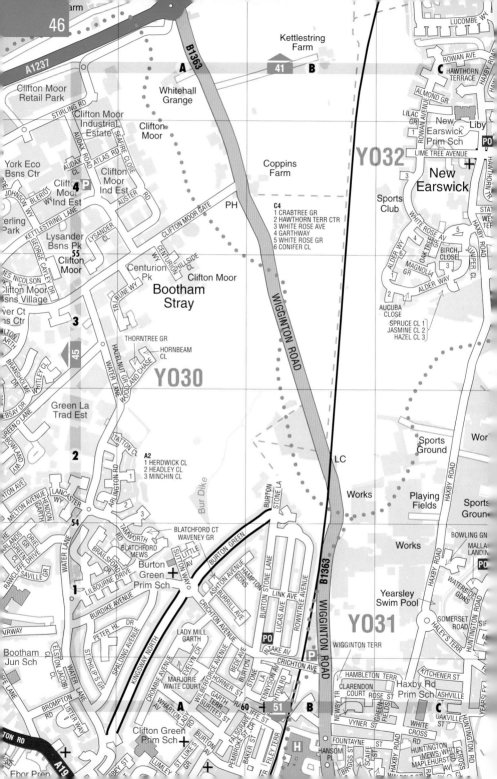

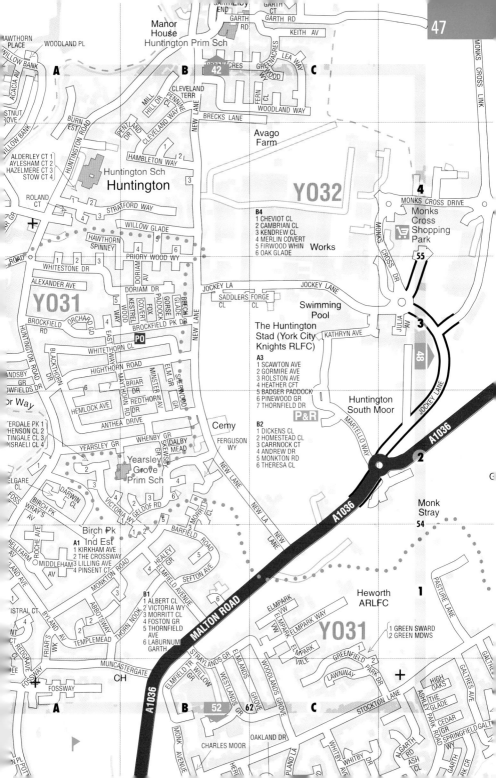

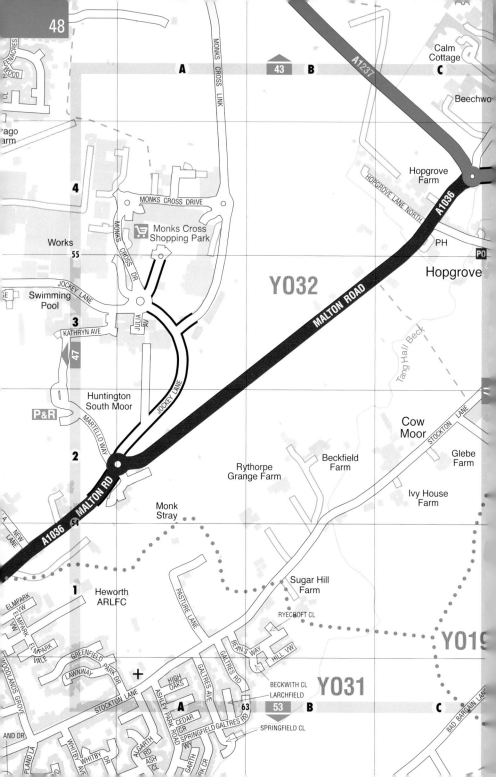

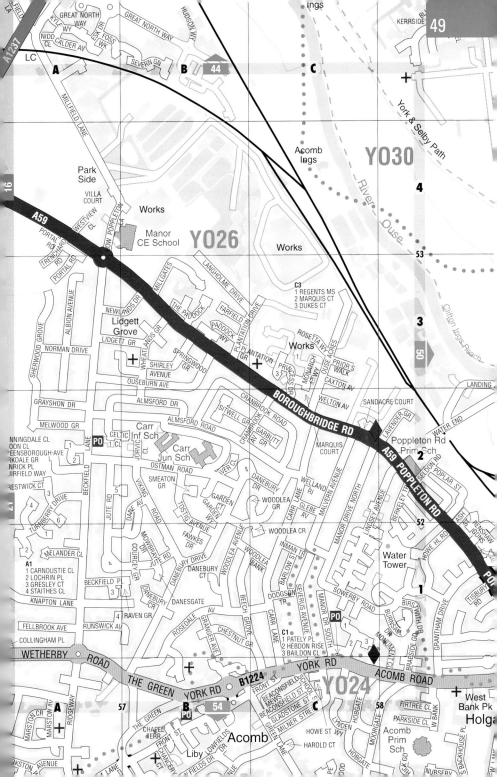

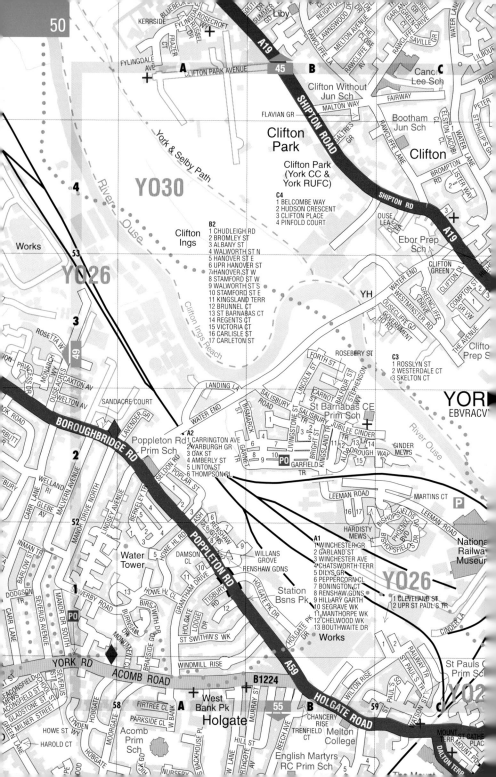

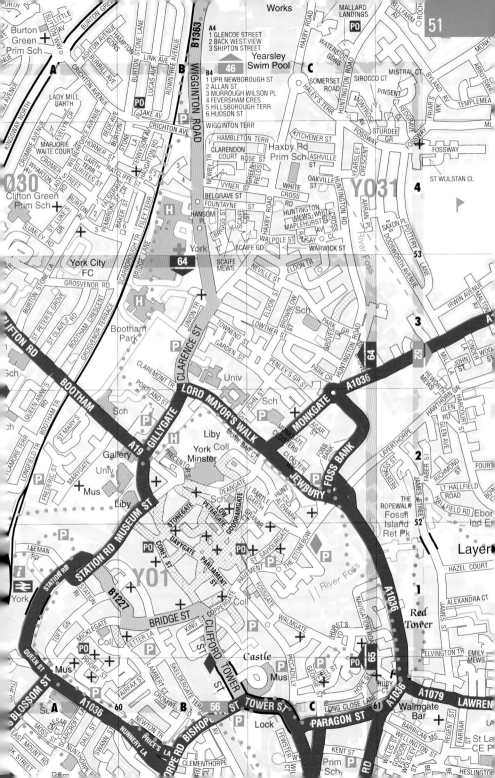

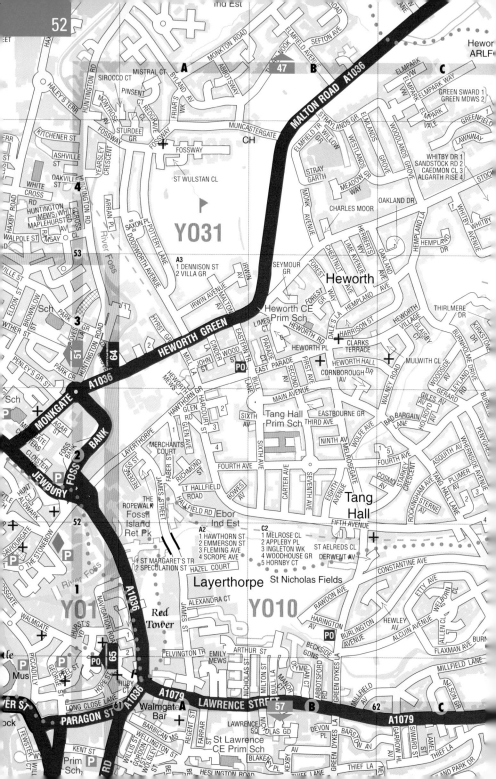

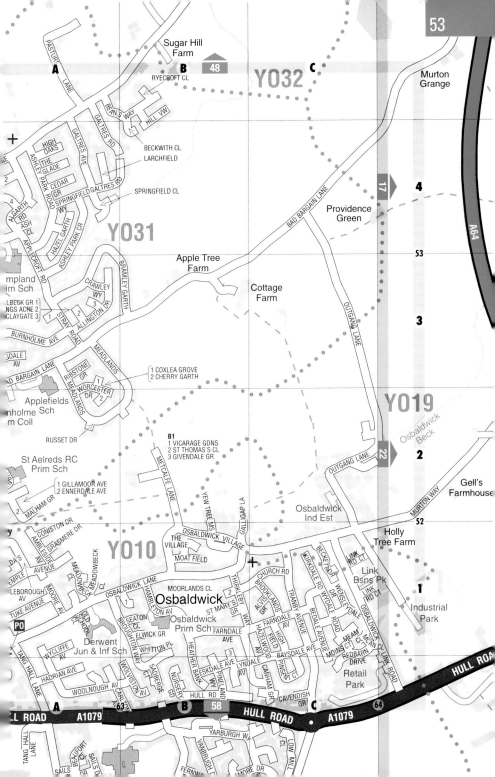

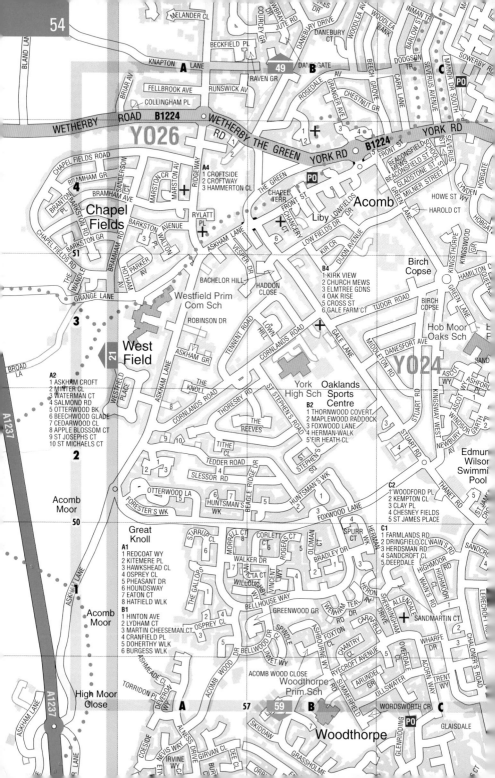

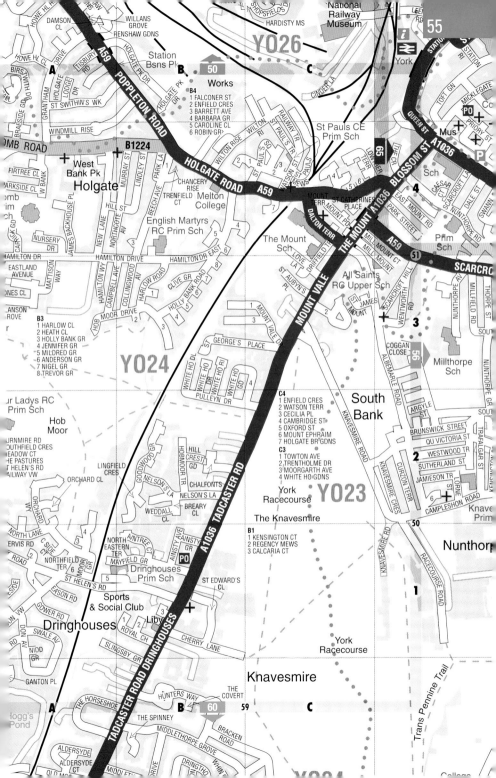

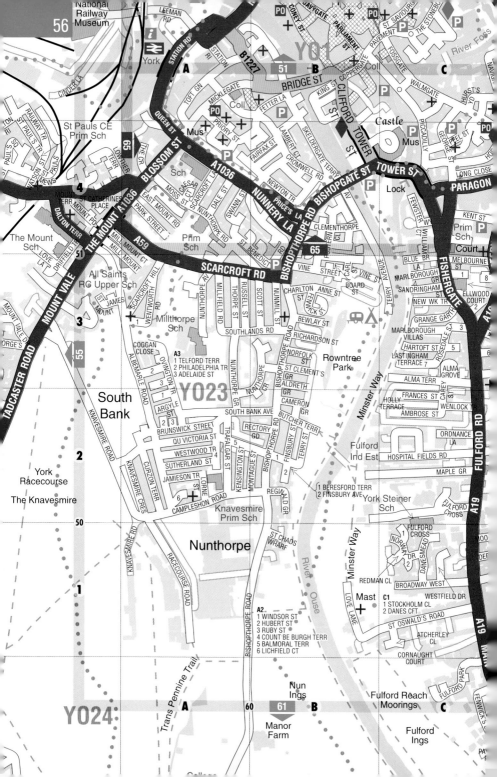

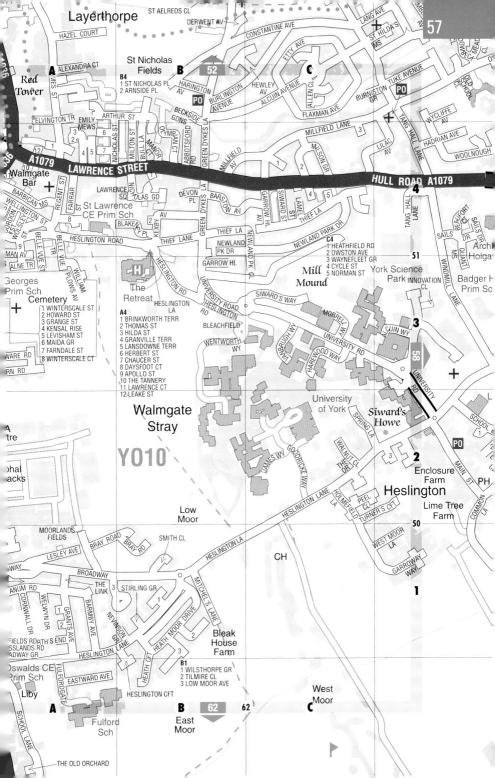

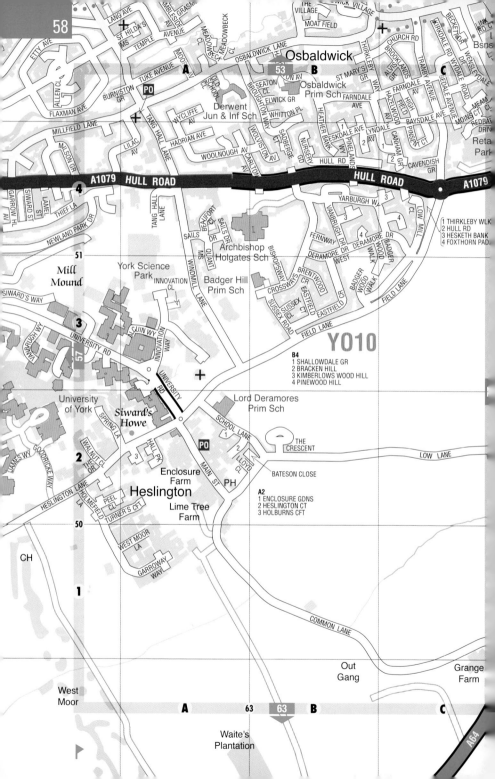

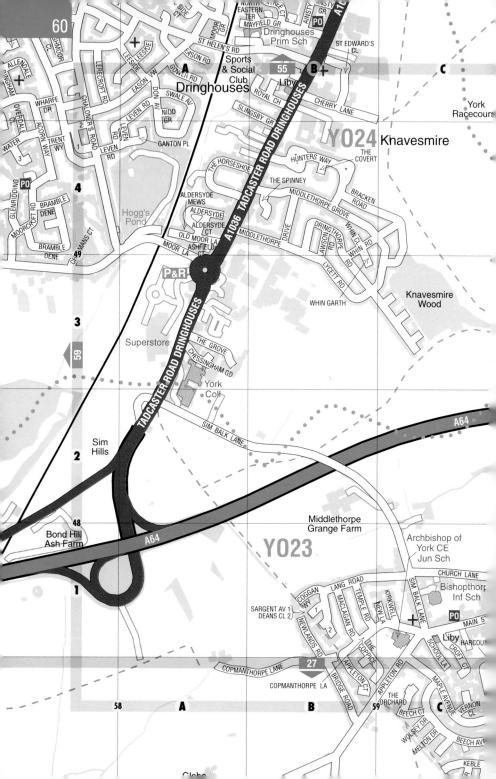

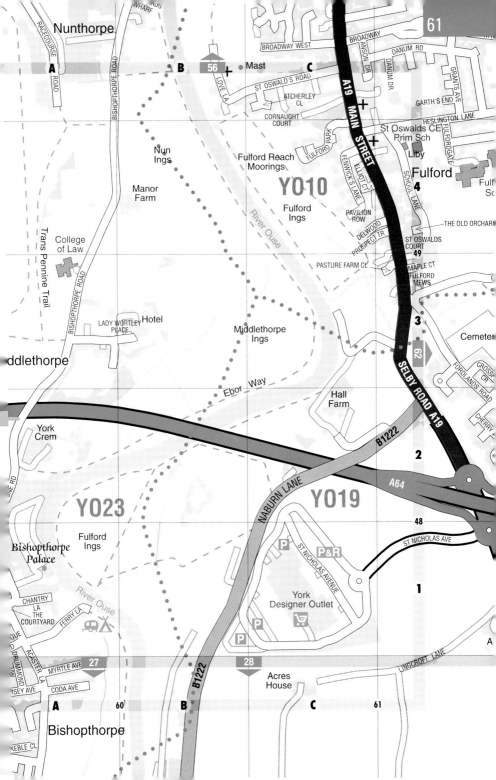

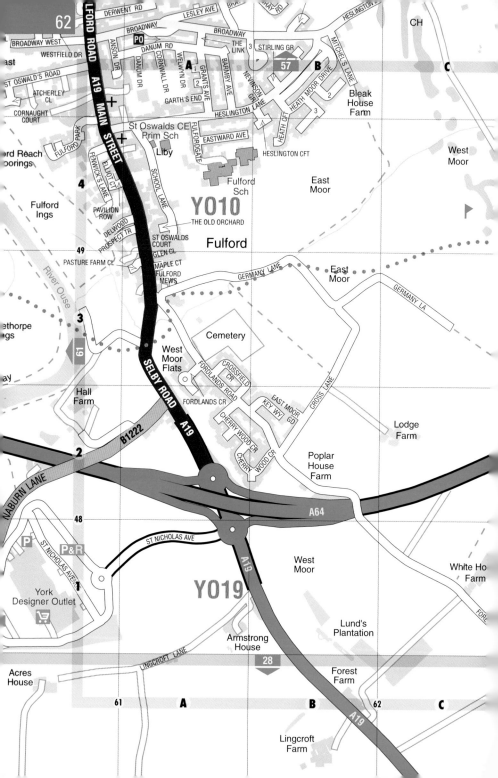

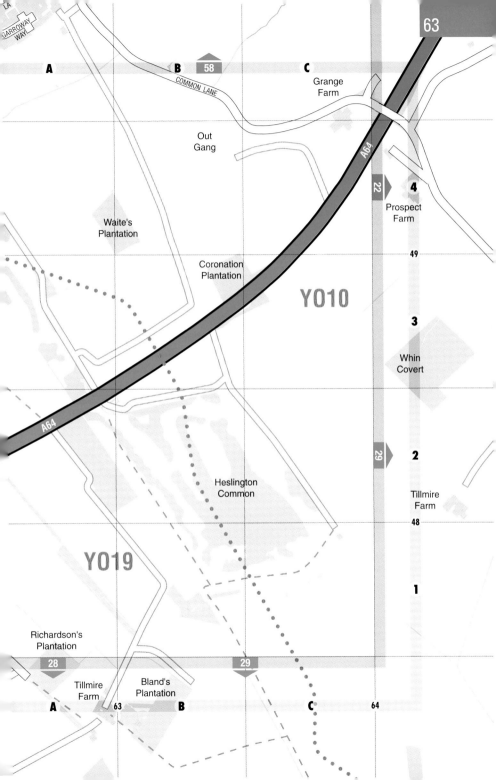

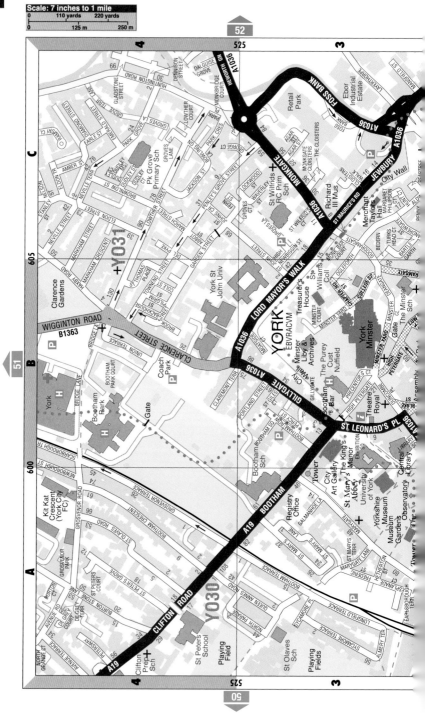

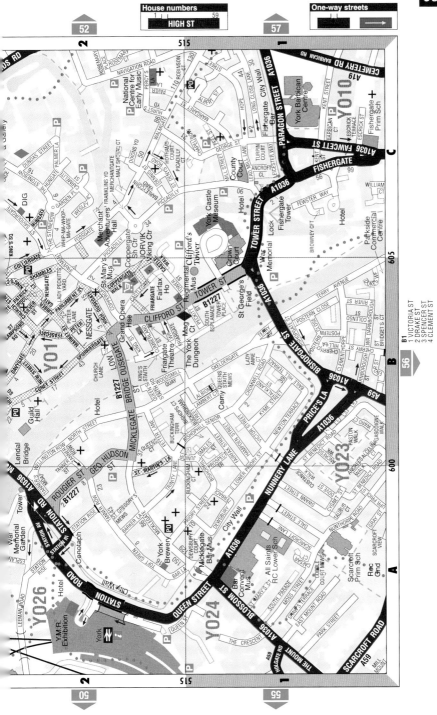

House numbers
1   59
HIGH ST

One-way streets

52
57

Index

Street names are listed alphabetically and show the locality, the Postcode District, the page number and a reference to the square in which the name falls on the map page

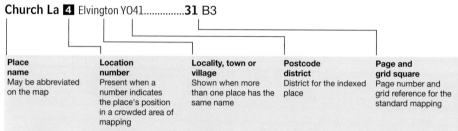

Church La **4** Elvington YO41..............**31** B3

Place name	Location number	Locality, town or village	Postcode district	Page and grid square
May be abbreviated on the map	Present when a number indicates the place's position in a crowded area of mapping	Shown when more than one place has the same name	District for the indexed place	Page number and grid reference for the standard mapping

Public and commercial buildings are highlighted in magenta. **Places of interest** are highlighted in blue with a star*
Cities, towns and villages are listed in CAPITAL LETTERS

Abbreviations used in the index

Ave	**Avenue**	Cres	**Crescent**	Gr	**Grove**	Mus	**Museum**	St	**Street**
Bldg	**Building**	Ct	**Court**	Ho	**House**	Par	**Parade**	Sta	**Station**
Bsns	**Business**	Ctr	**Centre**	Hospl	**Hospital**	Pk	**Park**	Terr	**Terrace**
Cl	**Close**	Dr	**Drive**	Ind	**Industrial**	Pl	**Place**	Wlk	**Walk**
Cnr	**Corner**	Ed	**Education**	La	**Lane**	Rd	**Road**	Yd	**Yard**
Coll	**College**	Est	**Estate**	Liby	**Library**	Sh	**Shopping**		
Cott	**Cottage**	Gn	**Green**	Mdw	**Meadow**	Sq	**Square**		

Index of streets, hospitals, industrial estates, railway stations, shopping centres, universities and places of interest

Abb–Bar

A

Abbey St YO30.... 50 C4
Abbotsford Rd
  YO10.......... 57 B4
Abbots Gait YO32. 42 B3
Abbot St YO31.... 64 C4
Abbotsway YO31.. 47 A1
Abelton Gr **33**
  YO32........... 11 A2
Acacia Ave YO32.. 42 A1
Acacia Gr **36**
  YO32........... 11 A2
Acaster La
  Acaster Malbis
  YO23........... 27 C2
  Acaster Selby
  YO23........... 33 C1
ACASTER
  MALBIS....... 27 C4
ACASTER SELBY. 34 A1
ACOMB........ 54 B4
Acomb Prim Sch
  YO24.......... 55 A4
Acomb Rd YO24 .. 55 A4
Acomb Wood Cl
  YO24.......... 59 B4
Acomb Wood Dr
  YO24.......... 59 A4
Acorn Way YO24.. 59 C4
Adelaide St **3**
  YO23........... 56 A3
Adlington Cl **8**
  YO32........... 11 C4
Agar St YO31..... 64 C3
Ainsty Ave YO24 .. 55 B1
Ainsty Gr YO24 ... 55 B1
Aintree Ct YO24 .. 55 B1
Airfield Ind Est
  YO41........... 30 B4

Albany St **3** YO26 50 B2
Albemarle Rd
  YO23........... 56 A3
Albert Cl **1** YO32. 47 B1
Albert St YO10.... 65 C1
Albion Ave YO26.. 49 A3
Albion St YO1.... 65 B1
Alcelina Ct YO23.. 65 B1
Alcuin Ave YO10.. 52 C1
Alcuin Way YO10. 58 A3
Aldborough Way
  YO26........... 50 B2
Alderley Ct YO32.. 47 A4
Aldersyde YO24... 60 A4
Aldersyde Ct
  YO24........... 60 A4
Aldersyde Mews
  YO24........... 60 A4
Alder Way YO32 .. 46 C3
Aldreth Gr YO23 .. 56 B3
Aldwark YO1 ..... 64 C3
Alexander Ave
  YO31........... 47 A3
Alexandra Ct
  YO10........... 52 A1
Alexandra Rd
  YO32........... 11 C3
Algarth Rd YO31.. 53 A4
Algarth Rise YO31 53 A4
Allanson Gr YO24. 55 A3
Allan St **2** YO30.. 51 B4
Allen Cl YO10..... 52 A1
Allendale YO24 ... 54 C1
Allerton Dr **22**
  YO26........... 16 B2
Allington Dr YO31 53 A3
All Saints RC Lower
  Sch YO23....... 65 A1
All Saints RC Upper
  School YO26 ... 56 A3
Alma Gr YO10 .... 56 C3
Alma Terr YO10... 56 C3
Almery Terr YO30. 64 C3
Almond Gr YO32.. 41 C1
Almsford Dr YO26 49 B2

Almsford Rd YO26 49 B2
Alness Dr YO24... 59 A4
Alne Terr YO10.... 57 A3
Alvin Wlk **9** YO41 31 A3
Alvis Gr YO10..... 53 C1
Alwyne Dr YO30 .. 45 A2
Alwyne Gr YO30 .. 45 A2
Amber Ct YO31.... 64 C4
Amberly St **4**
  YO26........... 50 A2
Amber St YO31 ... 64 C4
Ambler's La YO30...9 B4
Ambleside Ave
  YO31........... 53 A1
Ambrose St YO10. 56 C2
Amy Johnson Way
  YO30........... 45 C2
Ancress Wlk YO23 65 A1
Ancroft Cl YO1 ... 65 C1
Anderson Gr **6**
  YO26........... 55 B3
Andrew Dr **4**
  YO32........... 47 B2
ANGRAM 25 B4
Angram Cl YO30 .. 45 A2
Angram La YO61... 2 A4
Annan Ct YO24 ... 59 B3
Anne St YO23..... 56 B3
Anson Dr YO10 ... 56 C1
Anthea Dr YO31 .. 47 A2
Apollo St **2** YO10 57 A3
Apple Blossom Ct **8**
  YO24........... 54 A2
Appleby Glade
  YO32........... 41 C4
Appleby Pl **2**
  YO31........... 52 C2
Applecroft Rd
  YO31........... 53 A4
Applefields Sch
  YO31........... 53 A2
Apple Garth **15**
  YO26........... 16 B2
Appleton Ct YO23. 27 B3
Appleton Rd YO23 27 C3

APPLETON
  ROEBUCK 33 B2
Appleton Roebuck
  Prim Sch **1**
  YO23........... 33 B2
Archbishop Holgates
  Sch YO10....... 58 A4
Archbishop of York
  CE Jun Sch
  YO23........... 60 C1
Arenhall Cl **10**
  YO32........... 11 A1
Argyle St YO23 ... 56 A2
Arlington Rd
  YO30........... 45 C2
Armstrong Way
  YO23........... 45 A4
Arnside Pl **2**
  YO10........... 57 B4
Arran Pl YO31..... 51 C4
Arthur Pl **6** YO30. 39 A2
Arthur St YO10.... 52 A1
Arundel Gr YO30 . 45 A2
Ascot Rd YO32.... 10 C2
Ascot Way YO10 .. 54 C1
Ashbourne Way
  YO24........... 54 A1
Ash Cl YO31...... 53 A4
Ashdale Rd **19**
  YO19........... 23 B4
Ashfield Ct YO24.. 60 A4
Ashford Pl YO24.. 54 C3
Ash La **8** YO32... 11 A2
Ashley Park Cres
  YO31........... 53 A3
Ashley Park Rd
  YO31........... 53 A4
Ashmeade Cl
  YO24........... 54 A1
Ash St YO26...... 50 A1
Ashton Ave YO30 . 46 A1
Ashville St YO31 .. 51 C4
Ashwood Glade
  YO32........... 41 B3

Askham Bog Nature
  Reserve* TO23 .. 59 B2
ASKHAM BRYAN. 26 B4
Askham Bryan Coll
  YO23........... 26 B3
Askham Bryan La
  YO23........... 26 C4
Askham Croft **1**
  YO24........... 54 A2
Askham Fields La
  YO23........... 26 B3
Askham Gr YO24.. 54 A3
Askham La
  Askham Bryan
  YO24........... 21 C1
  Woodthorpe YO23 21 C1
  York YO24...... 54 A2
ASKHAM
  RICHARD..... 25 C4
Aspen Cl **3** YO19. 23 B4
Asquith Ave YO31. 52 C2
Atcherley Cl YO10 56 C1
Atlas Rd YO30 .... 45 C4
Aucuba Cl YO32 .. 46 C3
Audax Cl YO30.... 45 C4
Audax Rd YO30 ... 45 C4
Auster Rd YO30... 46 A4
Avenue Rd YO30.. 64 A4
Avenue Terr YO30. 64 A4
Avenue The
  32 Haxby YO32... 11 A1
  5 Haxby YO32.... 11 A2
  Rufforth YO23... 20 B3
  York YO30...... 50 C3
Aviator Ct YO30... 45 B4
Avon Dr YO32..... 42 B3
Aylesham Ct YO32 47 A4

B

Bachelor Hill
  YO24........... 54 B3
Backhouse St
  YO31........... 64 B4

Back La
  Appleton Roebuck
  YO23........... 33 C2
  Bilbrough YO23... 25 C2
  Copmanthorpe
  YO23........... 26 C2
  Cottingwith YO42 .. 38 B2
  11 Haxby YO32... 10 C2
  Holtby YO19 .... 18 A1
  Newton-on-Ouse
  YO30........... 8 A3
  York YO26...... 21 C4
Back Lane S YO19 37 B4
Back West View **2**
  YO30........... 51 A4
Bad Bargain La
  YO31........... 52 C2
Badger Hill Prim Sch
  YO10........... 58 A3
Badger Paddock **5**
  YO31........... 47 A3
Badger Wood Wlk
  YO10........... 58 C4
Baildon Cl **3**
  YO26........... 49 C1
Baile Hill Terr
  YO1............ 65 B1
Baker St YO30.... 51 B4
Balfour St YO26 .. 50 B2
Balfour Way YO32 11 C3
Balmoral Terr **5**
  YO23........... 56 A2
Bankside Cl **3**
  YO26........... 16 B2
Bannisdale **6**
  YO24........... 59 B4
Barbara Gr **4**
  YO24........... 55 B4
Barbers Dr
  17 Copmanthorpe
  YO23........... 26 C3
  Copmanthorpe
  YO23........... 59 A3
Barbican Ct YO10. 65 C1

Barbican Mews
YO10. . . . . 57 A4
Barbican Rd YO10 65 C1
Bar Convent Mus*
YO24. . . . . 65 A1
Barden Ct 6
YO30. . . . . 45 B2
Barfield Rd YO31 . 47 B1
Barker La YO1. . . . . 65 A2
Barkston Ave
YO26. . . . . 54 A4
Barkston Cl 3
YO26. . . . . 21 C3
Barkston Gr 6
YO26. . . . . 21 C3
Barkston Rd YO26 21 C3
Bar La YO1. . . . . . . 65 A2
Barleycorn Yd
YO1. . . . . 65 C2
Barley Hall* YO1 . 64 B3
Barley Rise YO32 . 11 C3
Barley View 16
YO32. . . . . 11 A1
Barlow St YO26 . . . 49 C1
Barmby Ave YO10. 57 A1
Barmby Cl 4
YO30. . . . . 45 B2
Barney La YO60. . . . 7 C2
Barnfield Way 7
YO23. . . . . 26 C2
Barons Cres YO23 26 C2
Barrett Ave 3
YO24. . . . . 55 B4
Barr La YO32. . . . . . 12 C1
Barstow Ave YO10 57 B4
Bartle Garth YO1 . 64 C3
Bateson Cl YO10. . 58 B2
Battleflats Way
YO41. . . . . 19 C3
Baysdale Ave
YO10. . . . . 58 C4
Beaconsfield Mews
YO24. . . . . 54 C4
Beaconsfield St
YO24. . . . . 54 C4
Beadle Garth 11
YO23. . . . . 26 C2
Beagle Croft YO41 19 B2
Beagle Ridge Dr
YO24. . . . . 54 C4
Beagle Spinney
YO41. . . . . 19 B2
Beanland La YO32 17 C4
Bean's Way YO31 . 48 A1
Beaufort Cl YO10 . 58 A4
Beaulieu Cl 1
YO32. . . . . 42 B2
Beaverdyke YO30 . 45 B2
Beck Cl 6 YO41. . . 31 A3
Beckett Dr YO10. . 53 C1
Beckfield La YO26 49 A2
Beckfield Pl YO26. 49 A1
Beck La YO19. . . . . 30 C1
Becks Cl 18 YO32. 31 A3
Beckside 7 YO41. 31 A3
Beckside Gdns
YO10. . . . . 52 B1
Beckwith Cl YO31. 53 B4
Bedale Ave YO10 . 53 C1
Bede Ave YO30 . . . 51 A4
Bedern YO1. . . . . . . 64 C3
Beech Ave
Bishopthorpe
YO23. . . . . 27 C3
4 Naburn YO23. . . 34 B4
York YO24. . . . . 55 B4
Beech Cl 2 YO41. 31 A3
Beech Cl 4 YO23. 27 C3
Beeches The
Skelton YO30 . . . . . 39 B1
26 Upper Poppleton
YO26. . . . . 16 B2
Beechfield YO30. . . 8 A3
Beech Glade
YO31. . . . . 47 B3
Beech Gr YO26 . . . 49 B1
Beech Pl 5 YO32. 11 C3
Beech Way 26
YO26. . . . . 16 B2
Beechwood Glade 6
YO24. . . . . 54 A2
Beeforth Cl YO32 . 41 C2
Belcombe Way 1
YO30. . . . . 45 B2
Belgrave St YO31 . 51 B4
Bell Cl 14 YO23 . . 11 A1
Belle Vue St YO10. 57 A4
Belle Vue Terr
YO10. . . . . 57 A4

Bellfarm Ave
YO31. . . . . 47 A1
Bellground La
YO30. . . . . 8 C1
Bell Hall* YO19 . . 35 A3
Bellhouse Way
YO24. . . . . 54 A1
Bellmans Croft 12
YO26. . . . . 22 C2
Bellwood Dr YO24 54 A1
Belmont Cl 3
YO30. . . . . 45 C2
Belvoir Ave 8
YO41. . . . . 31 A3
BENINGBROUGH. . 8 C1
Beningbrough Hall &
Gdns* YO30. . . . . . . 8 A2
Beningbrough La
YO30. . . . . 8 C2
Benjy La YO19 . . . . 37 A4
Beresford Terr
YO23. . . . . 56 B2
Berkeley Terr
YO26. . . . . 19 A3
Beverley Balk
YO24. . . . . 54 A1
Bewlay St YO23. . . 56 B3
BILBROUGH 26 C2
Bilsdale YO30. . . . . 45 A3
Birch Cl YO32. . . . . 46 C4
Birch Copse YO24 54 C3
Birch La 13 YO32 . 31 A3
Birch Park Ind Est
YO31. . . . . 47 A2
Birch Pk YO31 . . . . 47 A2
Birkdale Gr 4
YO26. . . . . 49 A2
Birker La YO41 . . . 24 C1
Birstwith Dr YO26 50 A1
Bishopgate St
YO23. . . . . 65 B1
Bishophill Jun
YO1. . . . . 65 A1
Bishophill Senior
YO1. . . . . 65 B1
Bishops Ct YO1. . . 65 B1
Bishopsfields Dr
YO26. . . . . 50 C2
Bishopsway YO10. 58 B4
BISHOPTHORPE . . 27 C3
Bishopthorpe Infant
Sch YO23 . . . . 60 C1
Bishopthorpe
Palace*
YO23. . . . . 61 A1
Bishopthorpe Rd
YO23. . . . . 61 A1
Bismarck St YO26. 50 A2
Black Dike La
YO26. . . . . 16 B1
Blacklee Cl 3
YO32. . . . . 6 A1
Blacksmiths Cl 5
YO41. . . . . 31 B3
Blackthorn Dr
YO31. . . . . 47 A3
Blake Ct YO19 . . . . 30 C1
Blakeley Gr YO30 . 45 B4
Blakeney Pl YO10 . 57 B4
Blake St YO1 . . . . . 64 B3
Bland La YO26. . . . 21 C3
Blatchford YO30 . . 46 A1
Blatchford Mews
YO30. . . . . 46 A1
Bleachfield YO10 . 53 B3
Blenheim Ct YO30 44 C4
Bleriot Way YO30 . 45 A4
Blossom St YO24 . 65 A1
Bluebeck Dr YO30 45 A4
Blue Bridge La
YO10. . . . . 56 C3
Blue Coat YO19 . . 22 C4
Blue Slates Cl
YO19. . . . . 30 C1
Board St YO23. . . . 56 B3
Bog La YO24. . . . . . 59 A3
Boltby Rd YO30. . . 45 B3
BOLTON PERCY. . . 34 C2
Bolton Percy Station
Nature Reserve*
YO23. . . . . 32 B1
Bond La YO23 . . . . 33 B2
Bonington Ct 7
YO26. . . . . 50 A1
Bootham YO30 . . . 64 A3
Bootham Bar*
YO31. . . . . 64 B3
Bootham Cres
YO30. . . . . 64 A4

Bootham Junior Sch
YO30. . . . . 50 C4
Bootham Park Ct
YO31. . . . . 64 B4
Bootham Park Hospl
YO31. . . . . 64 B4
Bootham Row
YO30. . . . . 64 B3
Bootham Sch
YO30. . . . . 64 A3
Bootham Sq YO30 64 B3
BOOTHAM
STRAY. 46 A3
Bootham Terr
YO30. . . . . 64 A3
Boothwood Rd
YO30. . . . . 45 A3
Bore Tree Baulk
YO19. . . . . 22 C3
Boroughbridge Rd
YO26. . . . . 49 C2
Borrowdale Dr
YO30. . . . . 45 B2
BOSSALL 14 C4
Bouthwaite Dr 13
YO26. . . . . 50 A1
Bowes Ave YO31. . 52 A2
Bowland Way
YO30. . . . . 45 C2
Bowling Green Ct
YO31. . . . . 46 C1
Bowling Green La
YO31. . . . . 64 C4
Bowness Dr YO30. 45 A2
Bowyers Cl
1 Copmanthorpe
YO23. . . . . 27 A3
Copmanthorpe
YO23. . . . . 59 B1
Bracken Cl YO32. . 42 B1
Bracken Hill 2
YO10. . . . . 58 B4
Brackenhills YO26 32 B2
Bracken Rd YO24 . 60 B4
Bradley Cres
YO23. . . . . 20 C3
Bradley Dr YO24. . 54 B1
Bradley La YO23 . . 20 B2
Braegate La LS24. 33 A4
Braeside Gdns
YO24. . . . . 55 A4
Brailsford Cres
YO30. . . . . 45 C1
Braithegayte
YO19. . . . . 30 B1
Bramble Dene
YO24. . . . . 59 C4
Bramham Ave
YO26. . . . . 21 C3
Bramham Gr 4
YO26. . . . . 21 C3
Bramham Rd
YO26. . . . . 21 C2
Bramley Garth
YO31. . . . . 53 A3
Brandsby Gr YO31 47 A3
Bransholme Dr
YO30. . . . . 45 C3
Branton Pl 5
YO26. . . . . 21 C3
Bravener Ct YO30. 8 A3
Bray Rd YO10. . . . . 57 B1
Breary Cl YO24 . . . 55 B2
Brecksfield YO30 . 39 B2
Brecks La
Strensall YO32 . . . . 12 A4
York YO32. . . . . 47 C4
Brentwood Cres
YO10. . . . . 58 B3
Briar Ave YO26 . . . 49 A1
Briar Dr YO31. . . . . 47 B3
Briars Ct YO23. . . . 33 A2
Briars Dr YO23 . . . 33 A2
Bridge Cl YO32. . . 41 B4
Bridge La YO30 . . . 64 B4
Bridge Rd YO23. . . 27 B3
Bridge St YO1 . . . . 65 B2
Bridle Way 1
YO26. . . . . 21 C3
Bridlington Rd 1
YO41. . . . . 19 C3
Briergate YO32 . . . 41 B4
Briggs St YO31 . . . 51 B4
Bright St YO26 . . . 49 C3
Brinkworth Rush
YO41. . . . . 30 C3
Brinkworth Terr 1
YO10. . . . . 57 A4

Broad Acres YO32 41 B4
Broad Highway
YO10. . . . . 30 B1
Broad La
Appleton Roebuck
YO23. . . . . 33 C3
Catton YO41 . . . . . 24 B4
Rufforth YO23. . . . 21 C2
Upper Poppleton
YO26. . . . . 15 C3
Broadlands YO10 . 30 C1
Broad Oak La 18
YO23. . . . . 11 A2
Broadstone Way
10 Rawcliffe
YO30. . . . . 45 A4
York YO30. . . . . 45 A4
Broadway YO10. . . 57 A1
Broadway Gr 3
YO10. . . . . 57 A1
Broadway W
YO10. . . . . 56 C1
Brockett Ind Est
YO23. . . . . 34 A3
BROCKFIELD 18 A3
Brockfield Park Dr
YO31. . . . . 47 B3
Brockfield Rd
YO31. . . . . 47 A3
Bromley St 2
YO26. . . . . 50 B2
Brompton Rd
YO30. . . . . 50 C4
Brooklands YO10 . 53 C1
Brook St YO31 . . . . 64 B4
Broome Cl YO32. . 42 B2
Broome Way
YO32. . . . . 42 C2
Brougham Cl
YO30. . . . . 45 B1
Broughton Way
YO10. . . . . 53 A1
Browney Croft
YO10. . . . . 65 C1
Brownlow St
YO31. . . . . 64 C4
Brown Moor 22
YO41. . . . . 19 C3
Brownmoor La
Huby YO61 . . . . 3 C3
Sutton-on-the-Forest
YO61. . . . . 4 A1
Brunel Ct 12 YO26 50 B2
Brunswick Cl 2
YO32. . . . . 6 B1
Brunswick St
YO23. . . . . 56 A2
Buccaneer Ct
YO41. . . . . 30 C4
Buckingham Ct
YO1. . . . . 65 A1
Buckingham St
YO1. . . . . 65 B1
Buckingham Terr
YO1. . . . . 65 A1
Bull La Huby YO32. 10 A4
York YO10. . . . . 57 B4
Bull Moor La YO60. 7 C1
Burdike Ave YO30. 45 B3
Burgess Wlk YO24 54 B1
Burlands La YO26. 21 B4
Burlington Ave
YO26. . . . . 49 B2
Burn Est YO32 . . . . 42 A1
Burnholme Ave
YO31. . . . . 53 A3
Burnholme Com Coll
YO31. . . . . 53 A3
Burnholme Dr
YO31. . . . . 52 C3
Burnholme Gr
YO31. . . . . 52 C3
Burniston Gr
YO10. . . . . 52 C1
Burnsall Dr YO26 . 50 A1
Burns Ct YO24 . . . 59 A4
Burrill Ave YO30 . . 46 A1
Burrill Dr YO30. . . 46 A1
Burton Ave YO30. . 51 A4
Burton Ct YO30. . . 44 C4
Burton Fields Cl 12
YO41. . . . . 19 C3
Burton Fields Rd 4
YO41. . . . . 19 C3
Burton Gn YO30 . . 46 A1
Burton Green Prim
Sch YO30. . . . . 46 A1
Burton Stone La
YO30. . . . . 64 A4

Burtree Ave YO30. 39 A1
Butcher Terr
YO23. . . . . 56 B2
Buttacre La YO23 . 25 C3
Buttercrambe Rd
Gate Helmsley
YO41. . . . . 19 B4
Sand Hutton YO41. 14 B2
Buttermere Dr
YO30. . . . . 45 A2
Butters Cl 20
YO23. . . . . 10 C2
Butt Hill 22 YO32 . 10 C2
Butts Cl 19 YO41. . 19 C3
Byland Ave YO31. . 47 A1
Byron Dr YO30. . . . 45 B1

C

Caedmon Cl YO31 52 C4
Caesar Cl YO24 . . 65 A1
Cairnborrow 4
YO24. . . . . 59 A4
Caithness Cl 1
YO30. . . . . 45 A4
Calcaria Ct 3
YO24. . . . . 55 B1
Caldbeck Cl 1
YO30. . . . . 45 C2
Calder Ave YO26. . 44 A1
Calf Cl YO32. . . . . . 11 A1
Calvert Ct YO32. . . 41 B4
Cambrian Cl 2
YO32. . . . . 47 B4
Cambridge St 4
YO24. . . . . 55 C4
Cameron Gr YO23 56 B2
Campbell Ave
YO23. . . . . 55 A3
Campleshon Rd
YO23. . . . . 56 A2
Canal Rd YO26 . . . 38 B2
Canham Gr YO10 . 58 C4
Canon Lee Sch
YO30. . . . . 45 C1
Canons St YO23 . . 27 C2
Canterbury Cl 9
YO32. . . . . 10 C2
Carey St YO10 . . . 56 C2
Carleton St 17
YO26. . . . . 50 B2
Carlisle St 16
YO26. . . . . 50 B2
Carl St YO23. . . . . . 56 B3
Carlton Ave YO10 . 58 A4
Carlton Rd YO41. . 31 B2
Carmelite St YO1 . 65 C2
Carmires Ave
YO32. . . . . 11 B2
Carnot St YO26 . . 50 B2
Carnoustie Cl 1
YO26. . . . . 49 A1
Caroline Cl 5
YO24. . . . . 55 B4
Carrbank La YO32 17 C3
Carrfield YO24. . . . 54 B1
Carrick Gdns
YO24. . . . . 55 A4
Carr Infant Sch
YO26. . . . . 49 B2
Carrington Ave 1
YO26. . . . . 49 B2
Carr Junior Sch
YO26. . . . . 49 B2
Carr La
Escrick YO19. . . . . 36 A2
Sutton-on-the-Forest
YO61. . . . . 4 C3
York YO26. . . . . 49 C2
Carrnock Ct 3
YO32. . . . . 47 B2
Carron Cres YO24 59 A4
Carter Ave YO31 . 52 B2
Castle Cl 1 YO32. 10 C2
Castlegate YO1. . . 65 B2
Castle Wlk YO1. . . 65 C2
Cat La YO23 . . . . . 25 C2
Cattal St YO26 . . . 50 B2
CATTERTON 25 A1
Cavendish Gr
YO10. . . . . 58 C4
Caxton Ave YO26 . 49 C3
Cayley Cl YO30 . . . 44 C4
Cecilia Pl 3 YO24 55 C1
Cedar Glade YO19 20 A4
Cedar Ct YO31. . . . 53 A4

Cedarwood Cl 7
YO24. . . . . 54 A2
Celtic Cl YO26 . . . 49 A2
Cemetery Rd
YO10. . . . . 65 C1
Centurion Pk
YO30. . . . . 46 A3
Centurion Way
YO30. . . . . 46 A4
Chaldon Cl 4
YO32. . . . . 11 C3
Chalfonts YO24 . . . 55 B2
Chaloner's Cres
YO24. . . . . 59 C4
Chaloner's Rd
YO24. . . . . 54 C1
Chancery Ct YO24 59 C4
Chancery Rise
YO26. . . . . 55 B4
Chantry Ave 14
YO26. . . . . 16 B2
Chantry Cl YO24. . 54 B3
Chantry Gap 11
YO26. . . . . 16 B2
Chantry Gr 13
YO26. . . . . 16 B2
Chantry La YO23. . 61 A1
CHAPEL FIELDS. . 54 A4
Chapel Fields Rd
YO24. . . . . 21 C3
Chapel La YO23. . . 26 B4
Chapel Row YO10. 65 A2
Chapel Terr YO24 . 54 B4
Chapman Cl 1
YO32. . . . . 6 B1
Chapmans Ct
YO30. . . . . 59 C3
Chapman's La
YO30. . . . . 9 A4
Chapter House St
YO1. . . . . 64 B3
Charles Moor
YO31. . . . . 52 B4
Charlton St YO23 . 56 B3
Chase Side Ct
YO24. . . . . 55 A1
Chatsworth Dr 16
YO32. . . . . 11 B2
Chatsworth Terr 4
YO26. . . . . 50 A1
Chaucer La YO31 . 6 A1
Chaucer St 7
YO10. . . . . 57 A4
Chaumont Way 1
YO32. . . . . 17 C3
Chelkar Way
YO30. . . . . 45 B2
Chelwood Wlk 12
YO26. . . . . 50 A1
Cherry Garth
YO31. . . . . 53 A2
Cherry Gr 16
YO26. . . . . 16 B2
Cherry Hill La
YO23. . . . . 65 B1
Cherry La YO24. . . 55 B1
Cherry Orch 7
YO32. . . . . 11 A1
Cherry Paddock
22 Haxby YO32. . . 11 A1
Kexby YO41. . . . . . 19 B3
Cherry St YO23. . . 65 B1
Cherry Tree Ave
Newton-on-Ouse
YO30. . . . . 8 A3
York YO32. . . . . 41 C1
Cherry Tree Dr 5
YO23. . . . . 34 A4
Cherry Wood Cres
YO19. . . . . 62 A2
Cheshire Ave
YO32. . . . . 11 C3
Cheshire Cl 6
YO32. . . . . 45 A3
Chesney Fields 4
YO24. . . . . 54 C2
Chessingham Gdns
YO24. . . . . 60 B1
Chessingham Pk
YO19. . . . . 23 B3
Chestnut Ave
YO31. . . . . 52 B3
Chestnut Ct YO32. 42 B2
Chestnut Gr
Acomb YO26 . . . . . 49 B1

Chestnut Gr *continued*
Huntington YO32... **42** A1
Chestnuts The 15
YO32............ **11** A1
Cheviot Cl 1
YO32............ **47** B4
Chiltern Way
YO32............ **42** B2
Chudleigh Rd 1
YO26............ **50** B2
Church Balk YO19 **23** A4
Church Cl
Askham Bryan
YO23............ **26** B4
5 Tollerton YO61... **2** A4
Wheldrake YO19... **37** C4
Church Farm Cl
YO23............ **20** B3
Churchfield Dr 28
YO32............ **11** A2
Church Gn 3
YO41............ **31** B3
Church La
Appleton Roebuck
YO23............ **33** B1
Bishopthorpe YO23. **60** C1
Bolton Percy YO23 . **32** C1
Catton YO41....... **19** C1
Dunnington YO19 .. **23** A4
4 Elvington YO41.. **31** B3
17 Haxby YO32..... **11** A2
Moor Monkton
YO26............ **15** A3
Nether Poppleton
YO26............ **44** A4
New Earswick
YO32............ **42** B2
Poppleton YO26 ... **16** C3
Skelton YO30 ..... **39** A2
10 Stamford Bridge
YO41............ **19** C3
Strensall YO32 .... **14** B1
Wheldrake YO19... **37** C4
York YO1......... **65** B2
Church Mews 2
YO26........... **54** B4
Church Rd
Stamford Bridge
YO41............ **19** C3
York YO10........ **53** C1
Church Rise YO19 **18** B2
Church St
20 Copmanthorpe
YO23............ **26** C2
Dunnington YO19 .. **23** A4
York YO1......... **65** B2
Cinder La
Upper Poppleton
YO26............ **16** C1
York YO26........ **50** B2
Cinder Mews
YO26........... **50** C2
City Art Gallery★
YO30............ **64** B3
Claremont Terr
YO31............ **64** B4
Clarence St YO31. **64** B4
Clarendon Ct
YO31............ **51** B4
Clarks Terr YO31. **52** B3
CLAXTON...... **14** A4
Claygate YO31... **53** A3
Clay Pl 3 YO24.. **54** C2
Clementhorpe
YO23............ **65** B1
Clement St 4
YO23............ **65** B1
Cleveland Gdns
YO32............ **17** C4
Cleveland St
YO24............ **50** C1
Cleveland Terr
YO32............ **42** B1
Cleveland Way
YO32............ **47** B4
Clifford St YO1 .. **65** B2
Clifford's Twr★
YO1............. **65** B1
CLIFTON....... **50** C4
Clifton Dale YO30. **50** C4
Clifton Gn YO30 .. **50** C4
Clifton Green Prim
Sch YO30....... **51** A4
Clifton Moor Bsns
Village YO30..... **45** C3

Clifton Moorgate
YO30........... **46** A4
Clifton Moor Gate
YO30........... **45** C3
Clifton Moor Ind
Estate YO30..... **45** C4
Clifton Moor Retail
Pk YO30........ **40** C1
Clifton Moor Sh Ctr
YO30........... **45** B4
Clifton Park Ave
YO30........... **45** A1
Clifton Park (York
CC & York RUFC)
YO30........... **50** C4
Clifton Pl 3 YO30 **50** C4
Clifton Prep Sch
YO30........... **64** A4
Clifton Rd YO30.. **64** A4
Clifton Without Jun
Sch YO30........ **45** B1
Clive Gr YO24.... **55** B3
Cloisters The
YO31........... **64** C3
Cloisters Wlk
YO31........... **64** C3
Close The
9 Acaster Malbis
YO32........... **34** B4
York YO30...... **45** B1
Cloverley Cl YO41. **19** B3
Cobble Court Mews
YO24........... **65** A1
Cobham Way
YO32........... **45** A4
COCK HILL..... **15** A3
Coda Ave YO23... **27** C3
Coeside YO24.... **59** A4
Coggan Cl YO23 .. **56** A3
Coggan Way YO23 **60** B1
Coledale Cl 2
YO30........... **45** B2
Colenso St YO23.. **65** B1
Cole St YO31..... **64** B4
College of Law
YO23........... **61** A1
College Rd YO23.. **26** C3
College St YO1 ... **64** B3
Colliergate YO1... **65** B2
Collier Hag La
YO23........... **25** A4
Collingwood Ave
YO24........... **55** B3
COLTON........ **33** A4
Colton La YO23... **33** A3
Common Croft La
YO26........... **16** A2
Common La
Dunnington YO19 .. **23** B2
Sutton upon Derwent
YO41............ **31** B1
Thorganby YO19 ... **37** B2
Warthill YO19 .... **18** B3
York YO10........ **58** B1
Common Rd YO19 **23** B4
Comon Rd YO60 .. **6** C2
Compton St YO30. **50** C3
Concorde Pk
YO30........... **45** C4
Coneycroft 10
YO19........... **23** B4
Coneygarth La
YO19........... **23** A2
Coney St YO1.... **65** B2
Conifer Cl 6
YO32........... **46** C4
Coningham Ave 1
YO30........... **45** A3
Coniston Cl 1
YO30........... **45** A2
Coniston Dr YO10. **53** A1
Connaught Way
YO32........... **42** B3
Constantine Ave
YO10........... **52** C1
Conway Cl 2
YO30........... **45** B2
Coombes Cl YO61.. **4** B4
Coopers Dr 15
YO23........... **26** C3
COPMANTHORPE
.... **27** A2
Copmanthorpe &
District Recreation
Ctr YO23........ **26** C2
Copmanthorpe La
YO23........... **27** B3
Copmanthorpe Prim
Sch YO23........ **26** C3

Copper Beech Cl
9 Dunnington
YO19........... **23** A4
Upper Poppleton
YO26........... **16** B1
Copper Beeches The
2 YO19......... **23** A4
Coppergate YO1.. **65** B2
Coppergate Sh Ctr
YO1............ **65** B2
Coppergate Wlk
YO1............ **65** B2
Coppice Cl 10
YO32........... **11** A2
Coppice The YO23 **60** B1
Copwood Gr 20
YO32........... **11** A1
Corban La YO32... **10** A3
Corban Way 21
YO32........... **10** C2
Corlett Ct
Woodthorpe
YO24........... **54** B1
York YO24....... **54** B1
Cornaught Ct
YO24........... **56** C1
Cornborough Ave
YO31........... **52** B3
Corner Cl 17
YO32........... **10** C2
Cornlands Rd
YO24........... **54** A2
Cornwall Dr YO10. **57** A1
Cornwood Way 30
YO32........... **11** A1
Cosmo Ave YO23.. **51** C2
Cotswold Way
YO32........... **42** C2
Coulson Cl 5 YO32 **6** B1
Count De Burgh Terr
YO23........... **65** A1
Courcey Gr YO26 . **49** B1
Courtneys YO19 .. **30** C1
Courtyard The
YO23........... **61** A1
Covert The YO24 . **60** B4
Cowper La YO23... **27** B1
Coxlea Cl YO31.... **53** A3
Crabtree Gr 1
YO32........... **46** C4
Cranbrook Ave
YO26........... **49** B2
Cranbrook Rd
YO26........... **49** B2
Cranbrooks The
YO19........... **30** B1
Cranfield Pl 4
YO24........... **54** B1
Crawley Way
YO31........... **53** A3
Crescent The
Kexby YO41....... **24** B2
1 Naburn YO23.... **34** B4
Stamford Bridge
YO41............ **19** C3
York YO24....... **65** A1
Crichton Ave
YO30........... **46** A1
Crinan Ct 3 YO32 **42** B3
CROCKEY HILL . **28** C2
Croft Ct YO23..... **60** C1
Croft Farm Cl 22
YO23........... **26** C3
Croftside 1 YO26. **54** A4
Croftway 2 YO31.. **54** A4
Crombie Ave
YO30........... **51** A4
Cromer St YO30 .. **51** A4
Crompton Terr
YO32........... **41** C3
Cromwell Rd YO1. **65** B1
Crookland La
YO32........... **11** B2
Crossfield Cres
YO19........... **62** A3
Cross La
Flaxton YO60..... **7** A1
Fulford YO19..... **62** B2
York YO24....... **65** A1
Crosslands Rd 2
YO10........... **57** A1
CROSS LANES .. **2** C4
Crossmoor La
YO32........... **11** A3
Cross St 5 YO24 . **54** B4
Crossways YO10 .. **58** B3
Crossway The 2
YO31........... **47** A1

Crummock 8
YO24........... **59** B4
Cumberland Cl 6
YO32........... **12** A3
Cumberland St
YO1............ **65** B2
Cumbrian Ave 4
YO32........... **12** A3
Cundall Cl 6 YO32 **.6** B1
Cundall Dr 6
YO32........... **34** B4
Curlew Glebe 8
YO19........... **23** A4
Curzon Terr YO23. **56** A2
Custance Wlk
YO23........... **65** A1
Cycle St 4 YO10.. **57** C4
Cygnet St YO23... **65** A1
Cyprus Gr 37
YO32........... **11** A2

D

Dalby Mead YO32. **47** B2
Dale Dike Gr
YO30........... **45** B3
Dale's La YO31... **52** B3
Dale St YO23..... **65** A1
Dalguise Gr YO31. **64** C4
Dalmally Cl YO24 . **59** A3
Dalton Hill YO19 .. **30** C1
Dalton Terr YO24 . **55** C4
Dam Hill YO23.... **20** A1
Dam La YO23..... **33** B1
Damson Cl YO26.. **50** A1
Dane Ave YO26... **49** B2
Danebury Cres
YO30........... **49** B1
Danebury Ct YO26 **49** B1
Danebury Dr
YO30........... **49** B1
Danes Croft 2
YO10........... **56** C1
Danesfort Ave
YO24........... **54** C3
Danesgate YO26.. **49** B1
Danesmead YO10. **56** C1
Daneswell Cl 3
YO41........... **19** C3
Danum Dr YO10 .. **57** A1
Danum Rd YO10.. **57** A1
Darbie Cl YO32 ... **41** C1
Darfield Cl YO32.. **6** A1
Darley Cl 7 YO41. **19** C3
Darling La YO23 .. **27** B1
Darnborough St
YO23........... **65** B1
Darnbrook Wlk
YO31........... **53** A2
Darwin Cl YO31... **47** A2
Dauby La YO31 ... **31** A4
Davygate YO1.... **65** B2
Daw La YO23..... **33** C2
Dawnay Garth
YO30............ **9** A2
Daysfoot Ct 8
YO10........... **57** A4
Deacons Ct 14
YO23........... **26** C2
Dealtry Ave 8
YO32........... **11** A1
Deangate YO1.... **64** B3
Deanhead Gr 7
YO30........... **45** B3
Deans Cl YO23.... **60** B1
Dee Cl YO24...... **59** A4
Deepdale 5 YO24 **54** C1
Deer Hill Gr YO30. **45** B4
Deerstone Way 22
YO19........... **23** B4
De Grey Ct YO30.. **64** A4
De Grey Pl 2
YO23........... **27** C3
DEIGHTON..... **35** C4
Deighton Grove La
YO19........... **28** C2
Delamere Cl 6
YO32........... **10** C2
Dell The YO30.... **39** A2
Del Pyke YO31.... **64** C4
Delwood YO10.... **61** C4
De Mowbray Ct
YO23........... **25** C4
Dennison St
1 York YO31..... **64** C4
York YO31....... **64** C4
Dennis St YO1.... **65** C2

Deramore Dr
YO10........... **58** B4
Deramore Drive W
YO10........... **58** B4
Derwent Ave
YO31........... **52** B1
Derwent Cl
East Cottingwith
YO42........... **38** B2
2 Stamford Bridge
YO41........... **19** C3
Derwent Ct YO41.. **19** B3
Derwent Dr YO19 . **37** B3
Derwent Est YO19 **23** A4
Derwent Infant Sch
YO10........... **53** A1
Derwent Junior Sch
YO10........... **53** A1
Derwent La YO19 . **23** A4
Derwent Pk YO19. **30** C1
Derwent Rd YO10. **53** A1
Derwent Wlk
YO32........... **42** B2
Deveron Way
YO24........... **59** A4
Devon Pl YO10.... **57** A4
Devonshire Ct
YO30........... **45** C2
Dewsbury Ct YO1. **65** A1
Dewsbury Terr
YO1............ **65** A1
Diamond St YO31. **64** C4
Dickens Cl 1
YO32........... **47** B2
Didsbury Cl YO30. **45** A3
DIG★ YO1....... **65** B2
Dijon Ave YO24... **54** B3
Dikelands Cl 19
YO26........... **16** B2
Dikelands La
YO26........... **16** B2
Dike Ray Cl YO32 . **46** A4
Dilys Gr 5 YO26.. **50** A1
Disraeli Cl YO32 .. **47** A2
Dixons Yd YO1.... **65** C2
Dodgson Terr
YO26........... **49** C1
Dodsworth Ave
YO31........... **52** A4
Doe Pk YO30..... **45** B3
Doherty Wlk YO24 **54** B1
Don Ave YO24.... **55** A1
Doriam Ave YO31. **47** B3
Doriam Dr YO31.. **47** B3
Dovecote Garth 5
YO41........... **31** A3
Dove St YO23.... **65** B1
Dower Chase
YO19........... **35** C3
Dower Pk YO19 .. **36** A3
Drakes Cl YO32 .. **42** B2
Drake St 2 YO23 . **65** B1
Drapers Croft 6
Copmanthorpe
YO23........... **26** C3
Copmanthorpe
YO23........... **59** A1
Driffield Terr
YO24........... **55** C3
Dringfield Cl 2
YO24........... **54** C1
DRINGHOUSES . **55** A1
Dringhouses Prim
Sch YO24....... **55** A1
Dringhouses Sports
Club YO24...... **55** B1
Dringthorpe Rd
YO24........... **55** A1
Drome Rd YO23 .. **27** A2
Drummond View
3 Bishopthorpe
YO23........... **27** C3
Bishopthorpe YO23. **61** A1
Dudley Ct YO31... **64** C4
Dudley Mews
YO31........... **64** C4
Dudley St YO31... **64** C4
Dukes Ct 3 YO26. **49** C3
Dukes Wharf
YO23........... **65** B1
Duncombe Dr
YO30............ **6** A1
Duncombe La
YO30............ **6** A1
Duncombe Pl YO1 **64** B3
Dundas St YO1... **65** C2
DUNNINGTON .. **23** B4

Dunnington Prim
Sch YO19....... **23** A4
Durlston Dr YO32. **11** C4
Dykelands Cl
YO19........... **37** B4
Dykes La YO23... **26** C2

E

Earfit La YO23.... **26** C1
Earle St YO31..... **64** C4
Earlsborough Terr
YO30........... **64** A3
EARSWICK..... **42** C4
Earswick Chase
YO32........... **42** B4
Earswick Village
YO32........... **42** B4
Eason Rd YO24... **55** A1
Eason View YO24 . **55** A1
Eastbourne Gr
YO31........... **52** B2
EAST
COTTINGWITH. **38** B2
Eastern Terr YO31. **52** A3
Eastfield Ave
YO32........... **41** B4
Eastfield Cres
YO10........... **58** B3
Eastfield Ct YO10. **58** B3
Eastfield La YO19. **18** B1
Eastholme Dr
YO30........... **45** A2
Easthorpe Dr 6
YO26........... **16** C2
Eastland Ave
YO23........... **55** A3
East Moor Gdns
YO19........... **62** B2
East Mount Rd
YO24........... **65** A1
East Parade YO31. **52** B3
Eastward Ave
YO10........... **62** A4
East Way YO31.... **47** A3
Eaton Ct 2 YO24.. **54** A1
Ebor Ind Est YO31 **64** C3
Ebor Prep Sch
YO30........... **50** C4
Ebor St YO23..... **65** B1
Ebor Way YO26... **16** C2
Eccles Cl YO30... **44** C3
Eden Cl YO24..... **59** B4
Edgware Rd YO10. **57** A2
Edmund Wilson
Swimming Pool
YO24........... **54** C2
Egremont Cl 11
YO41........... **19** C3
Eighth Ave YO31.. **52** B2
Elder Gr 38 YO32. **11** A2
Eldon St YO31.... **64** C4
Eldon Terr YO31.. **64** C4
Eldwick Cl YO30 .. **45** B3
Elgar Cl YO31..... **47** A2
Elliot Ct YO10.... **61** C4
Ellwood Ct YO10.. **56** C3
Elma Gr 3 YO30.. **45** A3
Elm Avenue 10
YO32........... **34** B4
Elm End 9 YO32 . **11** A2
Elmfield Ave YO31 **47** B1
Elmfield Terr
YO31........... **52** B4
Elm Gr YO31..... **47** B3
Elmlands Gr YO31 **47** B1
Elmpark Vale
YO31........... **47** C1
Elmpark View
YO31........... **47** C1
Elmpark Way
YO31........... **47** C1
Elms The YO32... **17** C3
Elm Tree Ave 9
YO26........... **16** B2
Elmtree Gdns 3
YO24........... **54** B4
Elston Cl YO30.... **45** C1
ELVINGTON.... **31** A3
Elvington CE Prim
Sch YO41....... **31** A4
Elvington Ind Est
YO41........... **30** C4
Elvington La YO23 **23** A2
Elvington Pk
YO41........... **30** C4

Elvington Terr
YO10 . . . . 52 A1
Elwick Gr YO10 . . . 53 B1
Embleton Dr 1
YO30 . . . . 45 B2
Emerald St YO31 . . 64 C4
Emily Mews YO10. 52 A1
Emmerson St 2
YO31 . . . . 52 A2
Enclosure Gdns 1
YO10 . . . . 58 A2
Endfields Rd 1
YO10 . . . . 57 A1
Enfield Cres 1
YO24 . . . . 55 C4
English Martyrs RC
Prim Sch YO32 . . 55 B4
Ennerdale Ave
YO31 . . . . 53 A2
ESCRICK 36 A2
Escrick CE Prim Sch
YO19 . . . . 36 C2
Escrick Ct YO19 . . 36 A2
Escrick Park Gdns
YO19 . . . . 36 A2
Escrick St YO10. . 65 C1
Eskdale Ave YO10. 58 B4
Esk Dr YO26 . . . . . 44 A1
Esplanade YO26 . . 65 A2
Esplanade Ct
YO30 . . . . 64 A3
Etive Pl YO24 . . . . 59 A4
Eton Dr 7 YO32 . . 10 C2
Etty Ave YO10 . . . 52 C1
Etty Cl 24 YO41 . . . 19 C3
Eva Ave YO30 . . . . 44 C3
Evelyn Cres YO30. 51 A4
Exhibition Sq YO1 64 B3

F

Faber Cl 20 YO23 . 26 C3
Faber St YO31 . . . . 52 A2
Fairfax 15 YO41 . . . 19 C2
Fairfax Cl YO23 . . . 32 C1
Fairfax Croft 19
YO23 . . . . 26 C2
Fairfax House *
YO1 . . . . 65 C2
Fairfax St YO1 . . . 65 B1
Fairfields Dr
YO30 . . . . 39 A2
Fairway YO30. . . . 45 C1
Fairway Dr 18
YO26 . . . . 16 B2
Falcon Cl 10 YO32 11 B2
Falconer St 1
YO24 . . . . 55 B4
Falkland St YO1 . . 65 B1
Falsgrave Cres
YO30 . . . . 51 A4
Farfield YO26 . . . . 49 B3
Farfield La YO19 . . 18 A1
Farmers Way
YO23 . . . . 26 C3
Farmlands Rd 1
YO24 . . . . 54 C1
Farmstead Rise
YO32 . . . . 41 C4
Farndale Ave
YO10 . . . . 53 C1
Farndale Cl 1
YO32 . . . . 11 B2
Farndale St YO10. 56 C3
Farrar St YO10 . . . 57 A4
Farriers Croft 6
YO23 . . . . 26 C3
Fawcett St YO10. . 65 C1
Fawkes Dr YO26 . . 49 B1
Feasegate YO1 . . . 65 B2
Fellbrook Ave
YO26 . . . . 49 A1
Fenwick's La
YO10 . . . . 61 C4
Fenwick St YO23. 56 B3
Ferguson Way
YO32 . . . . 47 B2
Fern Cl YO32 . . . . . 42 C1
Fern St YO31 . . . . . 64 C4
Fernway YO10 . . . 58 B4
Ferry Farm Cl 2
YO19 . . . . 27 C1
Ferry La
Bishopthorpe
YO23 . . . . 61 A1
Thorganby YO19 . . 38 A2

Ferrymans Wlk
YO26 . . . . 16 B3
Fetter La YO1 . . . . 65 B2
Feversham Cres 4
YO31 . . . . 51 B4
Fewster Way
YO10 . . . . 65 C1
Fewston Dr 9
YO30 . . . . 45 B2
Field La YO10. . . . 58 B3
Field View YO31 . . 52 B4
Fifth Ave YO31 . . . 52 B1
Filey Terr YO30 . . 51 B4
Finsbury Ave
YO23 . . . . 56 B2
Finsbury St YO23. 56 B2
Firbank Cl 9
YO32 . . . . 11 C4
Fir Heath Cl 5
YO24 . . . . 54 B2
First Ave YO31 . . . 52 B3
Firtree Cl
YO32 . . . . 42 B4
York YO24 . . . . 55 A4
Firwood Whin 5
YO31 . . . . 47 B4
Fishergate YO10 . . 65 C1
Fishergate Prim Sch
YO10 . . . . 65 C1
Flavian Gr YO30 . . 45 B1
Flaxman Ave
YO10 . . . . 52 C1
Flaxman Croft
YO23 . . . . 26 C3
FLAXTON 7 B2
Flaxton Rd YO32 . 12 A4
Fleet Bank La YO61 23 B2
Fleming Ave 3
YO31 . . . . 52 A2
Fletcher Ct 14
YO32 . . . . 11 A2
Fletcher's Croft 8
YO23 . . . . 27 A3
Florence Gr YO30. 44 C3
Fold Wlk YO32. . . . 6 A1
Folks Cl 13 YO32 . 11 B2
Fordlands Cres
YO19 . . . . 62 A2
Fordlands Rd
YO19 . . . . 62 A2
Foresters Wlk
YO41 . . . . 19 B2
Forester's Wlk
YO24 . . . . 54 A2
Forestgate YO32. 41 B4
Forest Gr YO31 . . . 52 B3
Forest La
Fulford YO19. . . . . 61 C1
Strensall YO32 . . . . 5 C1
Forest of Galtres
Prim Sch YO30 . . . 9 B2
Forest Way YO31 . 52 B3
Forge Cl
Huntington YO32. . 47 C3
Wheldrake YO19 . . . 37 C4
Forge La YO19 . . . 35 C4
Forth St YO26 . . . . 50 B3
Foss Bank YO31 . . 64 C3
Foss Ct YO31 . . . . . 47 A2
Foss Field La
YO23 . . . . 27 A1
Fossgate YO1. . . . 65 C2
Foss Islands Rd
YO31 . . . . 64 C3
Fossland View 4
YO32 . . . . 11 C4
Fossway
Stamford Bridge
YO41 . . . . 19 C2
York YO31 . . . . 51 C4
Foss Wlk YO26 . . . 49 A1
Foston CE Prim Sch
YO60. . . . . 7 C4
Foston Gr 4
YO31 . . . . 47 B1
Fountayne St
YO31 . . . . 51 B4
Fourth Ave YO31. 52 B2
Fox Covert YO31. . 47 B3
Foxcroft 3 YO30 . 47 A2
Fox Garth YO26 . . 16 C3
Fox Glade YO41 . . 19 B3
Foxthorn Paddock
YO10 . . . . 58 C4
Foxton Cl YO24 . . . 54 B1

Foxwood La 3
YO24 . . . . 54 B2
Frances St YO10 . . 56 C2
Frazer Ct YO30 . . . 45 A1
Frederic St YO30 . 64 A3
Friargate YO1 . . . . 65 B2
Friargate Theatre
YO1 . . . . 65 B2
Friar's Wlk YO31 . 47 A1
Front St
Naburn YO19 . . . . . 27 C1
York YO24 . . . . 54 B4
FULFORD. 62 B1
Fulford Cross
YO10 . . . . 56 C2
Fulfordgate YO10. 62 A4
Fulford Ind Est
YO10 . . . . 56 B2
Fulford Mews
YO10 . . . . 62 A3
Fulford Pk YO10 . . 61 C4
Fulford Rd YO10. . 56 C1
Fulford Sch YO10. 62 A4
Furlong Rd 23
YO41 . . . . 19 C3
Furness Dr YO30. . 45 A2
Furnwood 2
YO32 . . . . 41 C4
Fylingdales Ave 6
YO30 . . . . 45 A2

G

Gable Pk YO23 . . . 20 B3
Gainsborough Cl
YO32 . . . . 6 A1
Gale Farm Ct 6
YO24 . . . . 54 B4
Gale La
Thorganby YO19 . . 37 B1
York YO24 . . . . 54 B3
Gale The YO19 . . . 34 C1
Galligap La YO10 . 53 B1
Gallops The YO24 . 54 A1
Galmanhoe La
YO30 . . . . 64 A3
Galtres Ave YO31 . 53 A4
Galtres Gr YO30 . . 50 B4
Galtres Rd YO31 . . 53 A4
Ganton Pl YO24 . . 60 A4
Garbett Way 10
YO23 . . . . 27 C3
Garburn Gr 3
YO30 . . . . 45 A2
Garbutt Gr YO26 . . 49 C2
Garden Ct YO26 . . 49 B2
Gardeners Ct 12
YO23 . . . . 26 C2
Garden Flats La
YO19 . . . . 23 A4
Garden Pl YO1. . . 65 C2
Garden St YO31 . . 64 B4
Garden Way YO26. 49 B2
Garfield Terr
YO26 . . . . 50 B2
Garland St 2
YO26 . . . . 50 A1
Garlands The
YO30 . . . . 45 C1
Garnet Terr YO26 . 50 A2
Garroway Way
YO10 . . . . 58 A4
Garrowby View 5
YO41 . . . . 19 C3
Garrow Hill YO10 . 57 B3
Garrow Hill Ave
YO10 . . . . 57 C4
Garth Ct YO32 . . . 42 C1
Garth End YO32 . . 42 B1
Garth Rd YO32 . . . 42 B1
Garths End 20
YO10 . . . . 21 B2
Garth's End YO10 . 57 A1
Garth Terr YO30 . . 51 B4
Garthway 4 YO32 46 C4
Gascoigne Wlk
YO23 . . . . 65 B1
Gatehead La
YO42 . . . . 38 C4
GATE HELMSLEY. 19 A3
Gateland Cl YO32 . 41 B4
Gay Mdws YO32 . . 17 C3
Geldof Rd YO32 . . 42 C3
Gennell La YO60. . . 7 A2
George Cayley Dr
YO30 . . . . 45 C4
George Ct YO31 . . 64 C3

George Hudson St
YO1 . . . . 65 B2
George St YO1 . . . 65 C1
Gerard Ave YO31 . 52 C2
Germany La
Fulford YO10 . . . . . 62 A3
Fulford YO19 . . . . . 62 B3
Giles Ave YO31 . . . 52 C2
Gillamoor Ave
YO31 . . . . 53 A2
Gillingwood Rd
YO30 . . . . 45 B4
Gillygate YO31 . . . 64 A3
Gipsey Cnr YO19. . 30 A4
Girvan Cl YO24 . . . 59 A4
Givendale Gr 3
YO10 . . . . 53 B1
Glade The
Escrick YO19 . . . . . 35 C3
York YO31 . . . . 53 A4
Gladstone St
Acomb YO24 . . . . . 54 C4
York YO24 . . . . 54 C4
York YO31 . . . . 64 C4
Glaisby Ct YO31 . . 52 C3
Glaisdale YO24 . . . 59 A4
Glaisdale Rd YO26 21 B4
Glebe Ave YO26. . 49 C2
Glebe Cl
Bolton Percy
YO23 . . . . 32 C1
Strensall YO32. . . . 12 A4
Glebe Way 26
YO32 . . . . 11 A2
Glen Ave YO31 . . . 52 A2
Glen Cl YO10 . . . . . 62 A3
Glencoe St 1
YO30 . . . . 51 A4
Glen Rd YO31 . . . . 52 A2
Glenridding YO24 . 59 C4
Godwinsway 18
YO41 . . . . 19 C3
Goodramgate
YO1. . . . . 65 B2
Goodricke Way 5
YO10 . . . . 57 C2
Goodwood Gr
YO24 . . . . 55 B2
Goose La YO61 . . . . 4 B2
Goose Track La
YO24 . . . . 55 B2
Gordon St YO10 . . 57 A4
Gormire Ave 2
YO31 . . . . 47 A3
Gorse Hill 1
YO19 . . . . 23 B4
Gorse Paddock
YO32 . . . . 47 B3
Gouthwaith Cl
YO30 . . . . 45 B3
Government House
Rd YO30 . . . . 50 C3
Gowans The YO61. . 4 B4
Gower Rd YO24. . . 55 A1
Grampian Cl 4
YO32 . . . . 42 B1
Granary Ct YO1 . . . 64 B3
Grand Opera House
York * YO1 . . . . . . 65 B2
Grange Cl YO30. . . 39 A2
Grange Garth
YO10 . . . . 56 C3
Grange La YO26 . . 21 C2
Granger Ave YO26 49 B1
Grange St YO10. . . 56 C3
Grantham Dr
YO26 . . . . 50 A1
Grants Ave YO10. . 57 A1
Granville Terr 4
YO10 . . . . 57 A4
Grape La YO1 . . . . 64 B3
Grasmere Dr
YO10 . . . . 53 A1
Grasmere Gr 5
YO30 . . . . 46 B2
Grassholme YO24. 59 B4
Grayshon Dr YO26 49 A2
Gray St YO23 . . . . 56 C3
Great North Way
YO26 . . . . 44 A1
Greenacres YO32 . 42 B1
Green Cl YO10. . . . 45 C1
Greencliffe Dr
YO30 . . . . 50 C3
Greencroft Ct 14
YO19 . . . . 23 B4
Greencroft La 17
YO19 . . . . 23 B4

Green Dike 23
YO32 . . . . 11 A1
Green Dykes La
YO10 . . . . 57 B4
Greenfield Park Dr
YO32 . . . . 52 C4
Greenfields YO31 . 51 C4
Greengales Ct
YO19 . . . . 30 C1
Greengales La
YO19 . . . . 30 C1
Green Hills YO60 . . 14 A4
Green La
Acomb YO24 . . . . . 54 C3
Appleton Roebuck
YO23 . . . . 34 A3
Cottingwith YO42 . . 38 B2
Rawcliffe YO30. . . . 45 C2
Wigginton YO32 . . . 10 C2
Green Lane Trading
Est YO30. . . . . 45 C2
Green Mdws
YO31 . . . . 52 C4
Greensborough Ave
3 YO26 . . . . 49 A2
Greenshaw Dr 37
YO32 . . . . 11 A1
Greenside 18
YO19 . . . . 23 B4
Greenside Cl 24
YO19 . . . . 23 B4
Greenside Wlk 23
YO19 . . . . 23 B4
Green Sward
YO31 . . . . 47 C1
Green The
20 Dunnington
YO19 . . . . 23 B4
1 Skelton YO30. . . 39 A2
2 Tollerton YO61. . . 2 A4
York YO26 . . . . 54 B4
Green Way YO32. . 42 B1
Greenway The 2
YO32 . . . . 41 B4
Greenwich Cl 5
YO30 . . . . 45 A4
Greenwood Gr
YO24 . . . . 54 B1
Gregory Cl YO30 . . 39 B2
Gresley Ct 3
YO26 . . . . 49 A1
Grey Cl YO61 . . . . . 4 B4
Greystoke Rd
YO30 . . . . 45 A2
Greystone Ct
YO32 . . . . 41 B4
GRIMSTON 22 B3
Grimwith Garth
YO30 . . . . 45 B3
Grosvenor House
YO30 . . . . 64 A4
Grosvenor Pk
YO30 . . . . 64 A4
Grosvenor Rd
YO30 . . . . 64 A4
Grosvenor Terr
YO30 . . . . 64 A4
Grove Gdns 12
YO26 . . . . 16 B2
Groves Ct YO31 . . 64 C3
Groves La YO31. . . 64 C3
Grove Terrace La
YO31 . . . . 64 C4
Grove The YO24. . 60 A3
Grove View YO30. 50 C3

H

Haddon Cl YO24 . . 54 B3
Hadrian Ave YO10 58 A4
Hagg La
Colton LS24 . . . . . . 26 A1
Dunnington YO19 . . 23 B3
Haggwood Wlk
YO19 . . . . 30 B2
Hag La YO42. . . . . 38 B1
Haley's Terr YO31 . 46 C1
Halifax Ct 7
YO30 . . . . 45 C2
Halifax Way YO41. 30 C4
Halladale Cl 1
YO24 . . . . 59 A4
Hallard Way 7
YO32 . . . . 12 A4
Hallcroft La YO23. 24 B4
Hallfield Rd YO31. 52 A2
HALL GARTH. 23 B3
Hall Pk YO10 . . . . 58 A2

Hall Rise 12 YO32. 11 B2
Hambleton Ave
YO10 . . . . 53 B1
Hambleton Terr
YO31 . . . . 51 B4
Hambleton View
10 Haxby YO32 . . . 10 C2
4 Tollerton YO61. . . 2 A4
Hambleton Way
YO32 . . . . 47 B4
Hamilton Dr YO24 55 A3
Hamilton Drive E
YO24 . . . . 55 B3
Hamilton Drive W
YO24 . . . . 54 C3
Hamilton Way
YO24 . . . . 55 A3
Hammerton Cl 3
YO26 . . . . 54 A4
Hampden St YO1 . 65 B1
Hampson Gdns
YO30 . . . . 46 A1
Hampton Gdns
YO30 . . . . 46 B1
Handley Cl YO30. . 45 C3
Hanover Street E 5
YO30 . . . . 50 B2
Hanover Street W 7
YO30 . . . . 50 B2
Hansom Pl YO31. . 51 B4
Harcourt Cl
1 Bishopthorpe
YO23 . . . . 27 C3
Bishopthorpe YO23. 60 C1
Wheldrake YO19. . . 37 B4
Harcourt St YO31 . 52 A2
Harden Cl YO30. . . 45 B3
Hardisty Mews
YO26 . . . . 50 C1
Hardrada Way 3
YO41 . . . . 19 C2
Harewood Cl
Rawcliffe YO30. . . . 44 C3
5 Wigginton YO32. 10 C2
Harewood Way
YO10 . . . . 57 C2
Harington Ave
YO10 . . . . 52 B1
Harland Cl YO61. . . 4 B4
Harlow Cl 1
YO24 . . . . 55 B3
Harlow Rd YO24 . . 55 B3
Harold Ct YO24 . . . 54 C4
Harolds Way 1
YO41 . . . . 19 C2
Harrier Ct YO41. . . 30 C4
Harrison St YO31 . 52 B3
Harrow Glade 5
YO30 . . . . 45 C2
Hartoft St YO10. . . 56 C3
Harvest Cl 11
YO32 . . . . 12 A4
Harwood Rd YO26 21 B4
Hassacarr La
YO19 . . . . 23 B3
Hastings Cl 4
YO30 . . . . 45 C2
Hatfield Cl 3
YO30 . . . . 45 A4
Hatfield Wlk 8
YO24 . . . . 54 A1
Hatters Cl 18
YO23 . . . . 26 C3
Haughton Rd
YO31 . . . . 51 B4
Hauling La YO23 . . 27 B1
Haverah Ct YO30 . 45 B2
Hawkshead Cl 3
YO24 . . . . 54 A1
Hawthorne Ave 12
YO32 . . . . 11 A2
Hawthorne Gr
YO31 . . . . 52 A2
Hawthorne Mews
YO32 . . . . 12 A4
Hawthorn Gr
YO31 . . . . 52 A2
Hawthorn Pl
YO32 . . . . 42 A1
Hawthorn Spinney
YO31 . . . . 47 A4
Hawthorn St 1
YO31 . . . . 52 A2
Hawthorn Terr
YO32 . . . . 41 C1

Hawthorn Terrace
Ctr 2 YO32...... 46 C4
Hawthorn Terrace N
YO32.......... 41 C1
Hawthorn Terrace S
YO32.......... 46 C4
HAXBY 41 C4
Haxby Moor Rd
YO32.......... 11 C4
Haxby Rd
Clifton YO31 ...... 46 C2
New Earswick
YO32.......... 41 C3
York YO31...... 64 B4
Haxby Rd Prim Sch
YO31.......... 51 C4
Hayforth Cl YO30. 45 C3
Hazel Cl YO32 .... 46 C3
Hazel Ct YO10 .... 52 A1
Hazel Garth YO31. 53 A4
Hazelmere Ct
YO32.......... 47 A4
Hazelnut Gr YO30. 46 A3
Hazelwood Ave
YO10.......... 53 C1
Headland Cl 30
YO32.......... 11 A2
Headlands Prim Sch
YO32.......... 11 A1
Headley Cl 2
YO30.......... 46 A2
Healey Gr YO31.. 47 B1
Heath Cl 2 YO24 . 55 B3
Heath Croft YO10. 62 B4
Heather Bank
13 Stamford Bridge
YO41.......... 19 C3
York YO10...... 53 B1
Heather Cl YO32. 42 C1
Heather Croft 4
YO31.......... 47 A3
Heathfield Rd 1
YO10.......... 57 C4
Heath Moor Dr
YO10.......... 57 B1
Heath Ride YO32 . 6 A1
Hebdon Rise 2
YO26.......... 49 C1
Height Lands La
YO23.......... 20 C3
Helmsdale YO24.. 59 B3
Helmsley Gr 16
YO32.......... 10 C2
Hemlock Ave
YO31.......... 47 A2
Hempland Ave
YO31.......... 52 B3
Hempland Dr
YO31.......... 52 C4
Hempland La
YO31.......... 52 C4
Hempland Prim Sch
YO31.......... 53 A3
Hendon Garth
YO30.......... 45 C2
Herbert St 6
YO10.......... 57 A4
Herberts Way
YO31.......... 52 B4
Herdsman Dr 7
YO23.......... 27 A3
Herdsman Rd 8
YO24.......... 54 C1
Herdwick Cl 1
YO30.......... 46 A2
Herman Wlk YO24 54 B1
Heron Ave YO24 .. 54 B1
Heron Rise YO32.. 42 B2
Hesketh Bank
YO10.......... 58 C4
Heslin Cl 12 YO32. 11 A1
HESLINGTON 58 A2
Heslington Croft
YO10.......... 62 B4
Heslington Ct 2
YO10.......... 58 A2
Heslington La
Heslington YO10.. 57 C2
York YO10...... 57 B4
Heslington Rd
YO10.......... 57 A4
HESSAY 15 B1
Hessay Ind Est
YO26.......... 15 B1

Hessay Pl 2
YO26.......... 21 C3
Hetherton St
YO30.......... 64 A3
Hewley Ave YO10 . 52 C1
HEWORTH 52 B3
Heworth YO31..... 52 C3
Heworth CE Prim
Sch YO31....... 52 B3
Heworth Gn YO31. 64 C4
Heworth Hall Dr
YO31.......... 52 B3
Heworth Mews
YO31.......... 52 A3
Heworth Pl YO31 . 52 B3
Heworth Rd YO31. 52 B3
Heworth Village
YO31.......... 52 C3
HIGH CATTON 19 C1
High Catton Rd
YO41.......... 19 C1
Highcliffe Ct
YO30.......... 50 C3
High Field YO10 .. 53 C1
High Garth YO32.. 42 C4
Highgrove Cl 7
YO30.......... 45 A4
High La YO41..... 31 C4
Highlands Ave 5
YO32.......... 12 A4
Highmoor Cl
YO24.......... 54 C1
High Moor La YO30 2 B1
Highmoor Rd
YO24.......... 54 C1
High Newbiggin St
YO31.......... 64 B3
High Oaks YO31 .. 53 A4
High Ousegate
YO1........... 65 B2
High Petergate
YO1........... 64 B3
Highthorn Rd
YO31.......... 47 A3
Hilbeck Gr YO31.. 53 A3
Hilbra Ave YO32 . 41 C3
Hilda St 3 YO10.. 57 A4
Hillary Garth 9
YO26.......... 49 C1
Hill Crest YO19 .. 18 B2
Hillcrest Ave
YO26.......... 16 C2
Hill Crest Gdns
YO24.......... 55 B2
Hillgarth Ct 4
YO41.......... 31 A3
Hillsborough Terr 5
YO30.......... 51 B4
Hillside Cl YO30 .. 46 A3
Hill St YO24 ..... 55 A3
Hill View YO31.... 53 B4
Hinton Ave 1
YO24.......... 54 B1
Hobgate YO24.... 54 C4
Hob Moor Dr
YO24.......... 55 A3
Hob Moor Oaks Sch
YO26.......... 54 C4
Hob Moor Prim Sch
YO24.......... 55 A3
Hobmoor Terr
YO24.......... 55 B2
Hobson Cl 4
YO23.......... 26 C2
Hodgson La YO26. 16 B1
Holburns Croft 3
YO10.......... 58 A2
HOLGATE........ 55 B4
Holgate Bridge Gdn
7 YO24 .... 55 A3
Holgate Lodge Dr
YO26.......... 50 A1
Holgate Park Dr
YO26.......... 50 B1
Holgate Rd YO24 . 65 A1
Hollies The YO19.. 17 C4
Hollis Cres YO32.. 12 A3
Holly Bank Gr 3
YO24.......... 55 B3
Holly Bank Rd
YO24.......... 55 B3
Holly Cl YO23..... 27 B1
Hollyrood Rd
YO30.......... 45 A4
Holly Terr YO10... 56 C2
Holly Tree Croft 4
YO19.......... 23 B4
Holly Tree Garth
YO32.......... 17 A4

Holly Tree La
Dunnington YO19 .. 23 B4
33 Haxby YO32... 11 A1
Holmefield La
YO10.......... 57 C2
HOLME GREEN .. 33 B1
Holme Green Rd
YO23.......... 33 B1
Holme Hill La
YO10.......... 22 B1
Holroyd Ave YO31. 52 C2
HOLTBY 18 B2
Holtby La
Holtby YO19 ..... 17 C2
Stockton on the Forest
YO19.......... 17 C2
Homefield Cl 5
YO23.......... 26 C2
Homelea YO23.... 11 C3
Homestead Cl 2
YO32.......... 47 B2
Hope St YO10..... 65 C1
HOPGROVE..... 48 C3
Hopgrove Lane N
YO32.......... 48 B4
Hopgrove Lane S
YO32.......... 17 B2
Hornbeam Cl
YO30.......... 46 A3
Hornby Ct 5
YO31.......... 52 C2
Horner St YO30... 51 A4
Horsegate Garth 25
YO32.......... 11 A2
Horseman Ave 24
YO23.......... 26 C3
Horseman Cl 2
YO23.......... 26 C3
Horseman Dr 25
YO23.......... 26 C3
Horseman La
YO23.......... 26 C3
Horseshoe The
YO24.......... 60 A4
Horsfield Way
YO19.......... 23 B4
Horsman Ave
YO10.......... 65 C1
Hospital Fields Rd
YO10.......... 56 C2
Hospitium The *
YO1........... 64 A3
Hotham Ave YO10 55 A2
Hothams Ct YO1.. 65 C2
Houndsway 6
YO24.......... 54 A1
Howard Dr YO30.. 45 A3
Howard Link
YO30.......... 44 C3
Howard Rd YO32.. 12 A3
Howard St YO10.. 56 C3
Howden La YO19 . 28 A2
Howe Hill Cl YO26 50 A2
Howe Hill Rd
YO26.......... 50 A1
Howe St YO24 .... 54 C4
Hubert St 2
YO23.......... 56 A2
Huby Ct YO10..... 57 A4
Huby Rd YO61..... 4 A4
Hudson Cl YO41 .. 19 C3
Hudson Cres 2
YO30.......... 50 C4
Hudson St 6
YO30.......... 51 B4
Hudson Way YO26 44 B1
Hull Rd
Osbaldwick YO10 .. 58 C4
York YO10...... 58 A4
Humber Dr 5
YO32.......... 12 A3
Hungate YO1..... 65 C2
Hunt Ct YO31..... 64 C3
Hunter Dr YO32... 30 C3
Hunters Cl
Dunnington YO19 .. 23 A4
27 Haxby YO32.. 11 A1
Hunters Way
YO24.......... 60 B4
Hunters Wood Way
21 YO19 ...... 23 B4
HUNTINGTON.... 47 A4
Huntington Mews
YO32.......... 51 C4
Huntington Prim Sch
YO32.......... 42 B1
Huntington Rd
YO31.......... 64 C4

Huntington Sch
YO32.......... 47 A4
Huntington Stadium
(York City Knights
RLFC) The YO32.. 47 C3
Huntsmans La
YO41.......... 19 B3
Huntsman's Wlk
YO24.......... 54 A2
Hurns La YO30.... 9 C1
Hurricane Way
YO30.......... 45 A4
Hurst's Yd YO1 ... 65 C2
Hutton Cl 3 YO26 16 C2
Hyrst Gr YO31 .... 52 A3

I

Ikin Way YO32.... 42 B3
Ilton Garth YO30.. 45 C3
Ingleborough Ave
YO10.......... 53 A1
Ingleton Wlk 3
YO31.......... 52 C2
Ingrish La YO23... 25 B2
Ings La
Cottingwith YO42 . 38 B2
Lillings Ambo YO32...6 B3
Nether Poppleton
YO26.......... 44 A2
Thorganby YO19 .. 38 A2
Tollerton YO61 .... 2 A3
Wheldrake YO19 .. 38 A4
Ings Rd YO19 .... 38 A1
Ings View YO30 .. 44 C3
Inman Terr YO26.. 49 C1
Innovation Cl
YO10.......... 58 A3
Innovation Way
YO10.......... 58 A3
Intake Ave YO30 . 46 B1
Intake La
Acaster Malbis
YO23.......... 34 B4
Dunnington YO19 . 23 B4
Invicta Ct YO24 .. 54 A1
Irvine Way YO24 .. 59 A4
Irwin Ave YO31 ... 52 A3
Iver Cl YO26...... 49 B2
Ivy Pl YO32....... 46 C4

J

Jackson St YO31.. 64 C4
Jackson's Wlk
YO23.......... 25 C4
Jacobi Cl YO30 ... 50 C4
James Backhouse Pl
YO24.......... 55 A4
James Nicolson Link
YO30.......... 45 C3
James St YO10 ... 52 A1
James Way YO10 . 57 C2
Jamieson Terr
YO23.......... 56 A2
Jasmine Cl YO32.. 46 C3
Jasmine Garth 6
YO41.......... 31 B3
Jaywick Cl YO32.. 6 A1
Jedwell Cl YO32.. 41 C2
Jennifer Gr 4
YO24.......... 55 B3
Jervis Ct YO41.... 31 B2
Jervis Rd YO24 ... 55 A1
Jewbury YO31.... 64 C3
Jockey La YO32... 47 B3
John St YO31..... 52 B2
Jorvik Cl YO26.... 49 B2
JORVIK Viking Ctr*
YO1........... 65 C2
Joseph Rowntree
Sch The YO32.... 42 A2
Jubber Gate YO1 . 65 B2
Jubilee Ct
35 Tollerton YO61.. 2 A4
35 Wigginton YO32. 11 A1
Jubilee Terr YO26. 50 B2
Julia Ave YO32.... 48 A3
Juniper Cl YO32.. 46 C4
Jute Rd YO26..... 49 A2

K

Kathryn Ave YO32. 47 C3
Keats Cl YO30 .... 45 B1
Keble Cl 11 YO23 . 27 C3
Keble Dr 12 YO23 . 27 C3
Keble Gdns YO23 . 27 C2
Keble Park Cres 13
YO23.......... 27 C3
Keble Park N
YO23.......... 27 C2
Keble Park S
YO23.......... 27 C2
Keepers Way 11
YO19.......... 23 B4
Keith Ave YO32 ... 42 C1
Keldale 4 YO32 .. 11 B2
Kempton Cl 2
YO24.......... 54 C2
Kendal Cl 6 YO19 23 B4
Kendrew Cl 3
YO32.......... 47 B4
Kenlay Cl YO32... 41 C1
Kennedy Dr 32
YO32.......... 11 A2
Kenrick Pl 5
YO26.......... 49 A2
Kensal Rise YO10. 56 C3
Kensington Ct 1
YO24.......... 55 B1
Kensington Rd
YO30.......... 44 C3
Kensington St
YO23.......... 56 A2
Kentmere Dr
YO30.......... 45 B2
Kent St YO10 .... 65 C1
Kerrside YO30 .... 45 A1
Kerver La YO19 ... 23 B4
Kestrel Wood Way
YO31.......... 47 B3
Keswick Way 5
YO32.......... 42 B2
Kettlestring La
YO30.......... 45 C4
Kexby Ave YO10 .. 57 B4
Kexby Stray YO41. 23 C2
Key Way YO19 .... 62 B2
Kilburn Rd YO10.. 56 C3
Kimberlows Wood
Hill 3 YO10.... 58 B1
Kinbrace Dr YO24. 59 A4
Kings Acre YO31.. 53 A3
Kingsclere YO32.. 42 B3
Kings Ct YO1..... 65 B2
Kingsland Terr 11
YO26.......... 50 B2
Kings Moor Rd
YO32.......... 17 C3
King's Sq YO1 .... 65 B2
King's Staith YO1.. 65 B2
King St YO1...... 65 B2
Kingsthorpe YO24 54 C3
Kingsway 6 YO41 19 C3
Kingsway N YO30. 51 A4
Kingsway W YO24 54 C2
Kingswood Gr
YO24.......... 54 C4
Kir Cres YO24 .... 54 B4
Kirk Balk La YO60. 14 A4
Kirkcroft 9 YO32.. 11 A1
Kirkdale Rd YO10. 53 C1
Kirkham Ave 1
YO31.......... 47 A1
Kirklands YO32... 12 A3
Kirkstone Dr
YO31.......... 47 A3
Kirkwell YO23 .... 60 C1
Kitchener St YO31 51 C4
Kitemere Pl 2
YO24.......... 54 A1
Kit Kat Crescent
(York City FC)
YO30.......... 51 A4
Kitty Garth YO19.. 37 C4
KNAPTON 21 C4
Knapton Cl 1
YO32.......... 12 A3
Knapton La YO26. 49 A1
KNAVESMIRE.... 60 C4
Knavesmire Cres
YO23.......... 56 A2
Knavesmire Prim Sch
YO23.......... 56 A2
Knavesmire Rd
Nunthorpe YO23 .. 56 A1

Knavesmire Rd
continued
York YO23........ 55 C2
Knoll The YO24.... 54 A3
Kyle Cl 3 YO61.... 2 A1
Kyle Way YO26 ... 44 A1
Kyme St YO1 ..... 65 B1

L

Laburnum Cl
YO23.......... 20 B3
Laburnum Farm Cl
YO26.......... 15 B1
Laburnum Garth 6
YO31.......... 47 B1
Laburnum Gr
YO19.......... 34 C1
Lady Anne Ct YO1 65 B1
Lady Hamilton Gdns
YO24.......... 55 A3
Lady Mill Garth
YO30.......... 46 A1
Lady Peckitts Yd
YO1........... 65 B2
Lady Rd YO30..... 51 A4
Ladysmith Mews 3
YO32.......... 11 C4
Lady Wortley Pl
YO23.......... 61 A3
Lakeside YO23.... 34 B4
Lakeside County
Prim Sch YO30 .. 45 B3
Lakeside Gr 1
YO32........... 6 A1
Lambert Ct YO1 .. 65 B1
Lamel St YO10.... 57 C4
Lamplugh Cres 9
YO23.......... 27 C3
Lancar Cl 18 YO32 10 C2
Lancaster Way
YO30.......... 45 C2
Landalewood Rd
YO30.......... 45 B1
Landau Cl YO30.. 45 B1
Landing La
22 Haxby YO32... 11 B2
York YO26....... 50 A3
Landings The 21
YO32.......... 11 B2
Lane The YO41.... 19 A3
Lang Ave YO10 ... 52 C1
Langdale Ave
YO31.......... 53 A3
Langholme Dr
YO26.......... 49 B3
Langley Ct 1
YO32.......... 42 B3
Lang Rd
Bishopthorpe
YO23.......... 60 B1
York YO32....... 42 B3
Langrickgate La
YO42.......... 38 B2
Langsett Gr YO30. 45 B4
Langton Ct 1
YO23.......... 11 C3
Langwith Stray
YO10.......... 29 B3
Lansdowne Terr 5
YO10.......... 57 A4
Lansdown Way 7
YO32.......... 11 B2
Lanshaw Croft
YO30.......... 45 B2
Larchfield YO31... 53 A4
Larch Way 35
YO32.......... 11 A2
Larkfield Cl 1
YO23.......... 26 C3
Lasenby Cl YO32.. 41 C2
Lastingham Terr
YO10.......... 56 C3
Laurel Cl YO32.... 42 C4
Lavender Gr YO26 50 A2
Laveracks Ind Est
YO41.......... 31 A4
Lawnswood Dr
YO30.......... 45 B1
Lawnway YO31 ... 52 C4
Lawrence Ct 11
YO10.......... 57 A4
Lawrence Sq
YO10.......... 57 A4
Lawrence St YO10 57 A4
Lawson Rd YO24.. 60 B4
LAYERTHORPE.... 52 A3
Layerthorpe YO31 64 C4

Leadley Croft 🔳
YO23 . . . . 26 C2
Lead Mill La YO1 . . 65 C1
Leake St 🔢 YO10 . . 57 A4
Learmans Way 🔳
YO23 . . . . 27 A3
Lea Way YO32 . . . 42 C1
Leeman Rd YO26 . 65 C1
Leeside 55 A1
Leicester Way
YO1 . . . . 65 C1
Leighton Croft 🔳
YO30 . . . . 45 B2
Lendal YO1 . . . . . . 65 B2
Lerecroft Rd
YO24 . . . . 54 C1
Lesley Ave YO23 . 57 A1
Leven Rd YO24 . . . 59 C4
Levisham St YO10 56 C3
Leyes The YO10 . . 53 B1
Leyfield Cl 🔳
YO32 . . . . 11 C4
Leyland Rd YO31 . 52 C2
Library Sq YO1 . . . 64 B3
Lichfield Ct 🔳
YO23 . . . . 56 A2
Lidgett Gr YO26 . . 49 A3
Lilac Ave
🔳 Appleton Roebuck
  YO23 . . . . 33 B2
🔳 Naburn YO23 . . . 34 B4
  York YO10 . . . . 58 A4
Lilac Gr YO32 . . . . 41 C1
Lilbourne Dr
YO30 . . . . 45 C1
Lilling Ave 🔳
YO31 . . . . 47 A1
Lilling La YO60 . . . 7 A4
Lilling Low La
YO32 . . . . .6 B3
Lime Ave YO31 . . . 52 B4
Limegarth 🔟
YO26 . . . . 16 B2
Limes Ct YO31 . . . 52 B3
Limes The YO32 . . 17 C3
Lime Tree Ave
YO32 . . . . 46 C4
Lime Tree Mews 🔢
YO19 . . . . 23 B4
Lincoln St YO26 . . 50 B2
Lindale 🔢 YO24 . . 59 B4
Linden Cl YO32 . . 42 B2
Linden Gr 🔳
YO30 . . . . 45 C1
Lindley Rd YO30 . . 45 B2
Lindley St YO24 . . 55 B4
Lindley Wood Gr
YO30 . . . . 45 A4
Lindsey Ave YO26 . 49 C1
Lingcroft La YO19 . 28 B3
Lingfield Cres
YO24 . . . . 55 B2
Link Ave YO30 . . . 46 B1
Link Bsns Pk
YO10 . . . . 53 C1
Link Rd YO32 . . . . 47 A3
Link Road Ct
YO10 . . . . 53 C1
Link The 🔢 Copmanthorpe
  YO23 . . . . 26 C3
  York YO10 . . . . 57 A1
Linley Ave 🔢
YO32 . . . . 11 B2
Linnet Way YO24 . 54 B1
Linton Rd 🔳
YO26 . . . . 16 C2
Linton St 🔳 YO26 . 50 A2
Lister Way YO30 . . 50 C4
Little Ave YO30 . . 46 A1
Littlefield Cl 🔳
YO26 . . . . 16 B2
Little Garth 🔳
YO26 . . . . 16 C2
Little Hallfield Rd
YO31 . . . . 52 A2
Little La 🔳 YO32 . . 11 A2
Little Mdws 🔢
YO32 . . . . 11 A1
Little Shambles
YO1 . . . . 65 B2
Little Stonegate
YO1 . . . . 64 B3
Littlethorpe Cl 🔳
YO32 . . . . .6 A1
Livingstone St
YO26 . . . . 50 B2
Lloyd Cl YO10 . . . . 58 A2

Lob La YO41 . . . . . . 19 C3
Lochrin Pl 🔳
YO26 . . . . 49 A1
Lockey Croft 🔳
YO32 . . . . 11 A1
Lockwood St
YO31 . . . . 64 C3
Lockyer Cl 🔳
YO30 . . . . 45 C1
Lofthouse La
YO41 . . . . 24 C4
Long Cl La YO10 . 65 C1
Longcroft 🔳
YO32 . . . . 11 A2
Longfield Terr
YO30 . . . . 64 A3
Long Furrow 🔢
YO32 . . . . 11 A1
Long La
  Catton YO41 . . . . . 24 C3
  Heslington YO10 . . 29 B4
Long Ridge Dr
YO26 . . . . 16 C2
Longridge Gdns 🔢
YO26 . . . . 16 B2
Long Ridge La 🔟
YO26 . . . . 16 C2
Longwood Link 🔳
YO30 . . . . 45 A4
Longwood Rd
YO30 . . . . 45 B4
Lord Deramores
  Prim Sch YO10 . . . 58 B2
Lord Mayor's Wlk
YO31 . . . . 64 B3
Lords La YO26 . . . 16 A2
Lords Moor La
YO32 . . . . 12 B4
Loriners Dr 🔢
YO23 . . . . 26 B4
Lorraine Ave 🔳
YO41 . . . . 31 A3
Love La
  Nunthorpe YO10 . . 56 B1
  York YO24 . . . . 55 C3
LOW CATTON . . 19 B1
Low Catton Rd
YO41 . . . . 19 A1
Low Croft 🔳
YO32 . . . . 11 B2
Lower Darnborough
  St YO23 . . . . 65 B1
Lower Friargate
YO1 . . . . 65 B2
Lower Priory St
YO1 . . . . 65 A1
Loweswater Rd 🔳
YO30 . . . . 45 A2
Low Farm Cl
  Huntington YO32 . . 47 C2
  York YO31 . . . . 52 B4
Low Fields Dr
YO24 . . . . 54 B4
Low Gn 🔢 YO23 . . 26 C3
Lowick YO24 . . . . . 59 B4
Low La YO10 . . . . . 58 C4
Low Mill Cl YO10 . 58 C4
Low Moor Ave 🔳
YO10 . . . . 57 B1
Low Moor La
  Askham Richard
  YO23 . . . . 25 C4
  Hessay YO26 . . . . . 15 B1
Low Ousegate
YO1 . . . . 65 B2
Low Petergate
YO1 . . . . 64 B3
Low Poppleton La
YO26 . . . . 49 A4
Lowther Cl YO31 . . 64 C4
Lowther St YO31 . . 64 C4
Lowther Terr
YO24 . . . . 55 C4
Low Well Pk YO19 . 37 B4
Low Westfield Rd
YO23 . . . . 26 B2
Loxley Cl YO30 . . . 45 B3
Lucas Ave YO30 . . 46 B1
Lucombe Way
YO32 . . . . 41 C1
Lumley Rd YO30 . . 51 A4
Lund Cl 🔢 YO32 . . 11 A1
Lundgreen La YO61 3 C4
Lundy Cl 🔟 YO30 . 45 C2
Lycett Rd YO24 . . . 60 B3

Lydham Ct 🔳
YO24 . . . . 54 B1
Lyndale Ave YO10 . 58 B4
Lynden Way YO24 . 54 C4
Lynwood Ave 🔳
YO23 . . . . 26 C3
Lynwood Cl YO23 . 11 C4
Lynwood View 🔳
YO23 . . . . 26 C3
Lysander Bsns Pk
YO30 . . . . 45 C4
Lysander Cl YO30 . 45 C4

M

Mcan Cl YO10 . . . . 53 C1
MacLagan Rd
YO23 . . . . 60 B1
Magnolia Gr YO32 46 C3
Maida Gr YO10 . . . 56 C3
Main Ave YO31 . . . 52 B2
Main St
  Appleton Roebuck
  YO23 . . . . 33 B2
  Askham Bryan
  YO23 . . . . 26 B4
  Bilbrough YO23 . . . 25 B2
  Bishopthorpe YO23. 60 C1
  Copmanthorpe
  YO23 . . . . 26 C2
  Cottingwith YO42 . . 38 B2
  Deighton YO19 . . . . 35 C4
  Elvington YO41 . . . . 31 B3
  Escrick YO19 . . . . . 36 A2
  Heslington YO10 . . . 58 A2
  Hessay YO26 . . . . . 15 A1
  Knapton YO26 . . . . 21 C4
  Nunthorpe YO10 . . 56 C1
  Poppleton YO26 . . . 16 B2
  Shipton YO30 . . . . . .9 B2
  Stamford Bridge
  YO41 . . . . 19 C3
  Sutton-on-the-Forest
  YO61 . . . . .4 B4
  Wheldrake YO19 . . . 37 B4
Malbys Gr 🔢
YO23 . . . . 26 C2
Malham Gr YO31 . 53 A2
Mallard Landings
YO31 . . . . 46 C1
Mallard Way 🔢
YO32 . . . . 11 B2
Mallory Cl YO32 . . 11 B2
Malt Kiln La YO23 . 33 B2
Malton Ave YO31 . 52 A3
Malton La YO60 . . . 7 C2
Malton Rd
  Huntington YO32 . . 47 C2
  York YO31 . . . . 52 B4
Malton Way YO30 . 45 B1
Malt Shoval Ct
YO1 . . . . 65 C2
Malvern Ave YO26 49 C2
Malvern Cl YO32 . . 42 B2
Mancroft 🔢 YO32. 11 A1
Manley Cl YO31 . . 42 B2
Manor Beeches The
🔳 YO19 . . . . 23 A4
Manor CE Sch
YO26 . . . . 49 B4
Manor Cl YO26 . . . 16 B1
Manor Ct
  York YO10 . . . . 57 B4
  🔳 York YO32 . . . . 42 B3
Manor Dr 🔢 YO19 23 A4
Manor Drive N
YO26 . . . . 49 C1
Manor Drive S
YO26 . . . . 49 C1
Manor Farm Cl 🔳
YO23 . . . . 26 C2
Manor Farm Ct
LS24 . . . . 33 A4
Manor Garth
YO32 . . . . 10 C1
Manor Heath
YO23 . . . . 26 B4
Manor La YO30 . . . 44 C3
Manor Park Cl
YO30 . . . . 45 A3
Manor Park Gr 🔳
YO30 . . . . 45 A3
Manor Park Rd
YO30 . . . . 45 A3
Manor Way YO30 . 45 A3
Mansfield St
YO31 . . . . 64 C3

Maple Ave YO23 . . 27 C3
Maple Ct
  Wheldrake YO19 . . . 29 C1
  York YO10 . . . . 62 A3
Maple Gr YO10 . . . 56 C2
Maplehurst Ave
YO31 . . . . 51 C4
Maplewood Paddock
🔳 YO24 . . . . 54 B2
March St YO31 . . . 64 C4
Margaret Philipson
  Ct YO1 . . . . 65 C2
Margaret St YO10. 65 C1
Marjorie Waite Ct
YO30 . . . . 51 A4
Market St YO1 . . . 65 B2
Markham Cres
YO31 . . . . 64 B4
Markham St YO31 64 B4
Marlborough Cl
YO10 . . . . 44 C4
Marlborough Gr
YO10 . . . . 56 C3
Marlborough Villas
YO10 . . . . 56 C3
Marmiam Dr 🔳
YO32 . . . . 17 C3
Marquis Ct 🔳
YO26 . . . . 49 C3
Marston Ave
YO26 . . . . 54 A4
Marston Cres
YO26 . . . . 54 A4
Martello Way
YO32 . . . . 47 C2
Marten Cl 🔳
YO30 . . . . 45 C1
Martin Cheeseman
  Ct 🔳 YO24 . . . . . . 54 B1
Martins Ct YO26 . . 50 C2
Marygate YO30 . . . 64 A4
Marygate La YO30 64 A3
Mask La YO41 . . . . 24 C1
Mattison Way
YO24 . . . . 55 A3
Mayfield Gr YO24 . 55 A1
Maypole Gr 🔳
YO19 . . . . 27 C1
Maythorn Rd
YO31 . . . . 47 A3
Maythorpe YO23 . 24 B1
Meadlands YO31 . 53 A3
Meadowbeck Cl
YO10 . . . . 53 A1
Meadow Ct 🔳
YO24 . . . . 55 A1
Meadowfields Dr
YO31 . . . . 46 C3
Meadow La 🔢
YO32 . . . . 11 A1
Meadows The 🔳
YO30 . . . . 39 A2
Meadow Way
  Heworth YO31 . . . . 52 B4
  Huntington YO32 . . 42 B1
Meam Ct YO19 . . . 36 A3
Melander Cl YO30 53 C1
Melander Gdns 🔳
YO32 . . . . 41 C4
Melbourne St
YO10 . . . . 56 C3
Melcombe Ave 🔢
YO30 . . . . 51 A4
Melrose Cl 🔳
YO31 . . . . 52 C2
Melrosegate YO31 52 B2
Melton Ave YO30 . 45 B1
Melton Coll YO24 . 55 B4
Melton Dr
🔢 Bishopthorpe
  YO23 . . . . 27 C3
  York YO30 . . . . 45 B1
Melwood Gr YO26 49 A2
Mendip Cl 🔳
YO32 . . . . 11 C4
Merchant
Adventurers' Hall✱
Merchantgate
YO1 . . . . 65 C2
Merchants Ct
YO31 . . . . 52 A2
Merchant Way
YO23 . . . . 26 C3
Merlin Covert 🔳
YO31 . . . . 47 B4
Metcalfe La YO19 . 53 B2
Micklegate YO1 . . 65 A2

Micklegate Bar
  Mus✱ YO24 . . . . . . 65 A1
Middle Banks 🔢
YO32 . . . . 11 A2
Middlecroft Dr
YO32 . . . . 11 C4
Middlecroft Gr 🔳
YO32 . . . . 12 A4
Middleham Ave
YO31 . . . . 47 A1
MIDDLETHORPE . 61 A3
Middlethorpe Dr
YO24 . . . . 60 A4
Middlethorpe Gr
YO24 . . . . 60 B4
Middleton Rd
YO24 . . . . 54 B3
Middlewood Cl
YO31 . . . . 20 B3
Midgley Cl 🔢
YO41 . . . . 19 C3
Midway Ave 🔳
YO26 . . . . 16 C2
Mildred Gr 🔳
YO24 . . . . 55 B3
Milestone Ave
YO23 . . . . 20 B3
Milford Mews 🔳
YO32 . . . . 41 C4
Milford Way 🔳
YO32 . . . . 41 C4
Millers Croft 🔟
YO23 . . . . 26 C3
Millfield Ave YO10 57 B4
Millfield Cl YO19 . 37 B4
Millfield Gdns
YO26 . . . . 16 C2
Millfield Ind Est
YO19 . . . . 37 B4
Millfield La
  Nether Poppleton
  YO26 . . . . 44 A1
  Poppleton YO26 . . . 16 C2
  York YO10 . . . . 57 C4
Millfield Rd YO23 . 56 A3
Millgates YO26 . . . 49 B3
Mill Hill YO19 . . . . 36 A2
Mill Hill Dr YO32 . . 42 B1
Mill La
  Acaster Malbis
  YO23 . . . . 27 B1
  Askham Richard
  YO23 . . . . 25 C3
  Haxby YO32 . . . . . . 10 C2
  York YO31 . . . . 52 A3
Mill Mount YO24 . 55 C4
Mill Mount Ct
YO24 . . . . 55 C4
Mill St YO1 . . . . . . 65 C2
Millthorpe Sch
YO23 . . . . 56 A3
Milner St YO24 . . . 54 C4
Milson Gr YO10 . . 57 C4
Milton Carr 🔳
YO30 . . . . 45 B2
Milton St YO10 . . . 57 B4
Minchin Cl 🔳
YO30 . . . . 46 A2
Minster Ave YO31. 47 B3
Minster Cl
  🔳 Haxby YO32 . . . 11 A1
  🔢 Wigginton YO32 . 11 A2
  York YO1 . . . . 64 B3
Minster Ct YO1 . . . 64 B3
Minster Sch The
YO1 . . . . 64 B3
Minster View 🔳
YO32 . . . . 11 C4
Minster Yd YO1 . . . 64 B3
Minter Cl 🔢 YO24 54 A2
Mistral Ct YO31 . . 47 A1
Mitchell La YO41 . 19 C1
Mitchell Way 🔢
YO30 . . . . 45 B4
Mitchel's La YO10 57 B1
Miterdale 🔢 YO24 59 B4
MLS Bsns Centres
YO30 . . . . 45 C3
Moat Field YO10 . . 53 B1
Moatside Ct YO31. 64 B3
Moins Ct YO10 . . . 53 C1
Moiser Cl YO32 . . . 41 C1
Monarch Way
YO26 . . . . 49 C3
Monk Ave YO31 . . . 52 B4
Monk Bar Ct YO1 . 64 B3
Monkbridge Ct
YO31 . . . . 64 C4

Monkgate YO31 . . 64 C3
Monkgate Cloisters
YO31 . . . . 64 C3
Monks Cross Dr
YO32 . . . . 47 C4
Monks Cross Link
YO32 . . . . 43 A1
Monks Cross Sh Pk
YO32 . . . . 48 A4
Monkton Rd 🔳
YO31 . . . . 47 B2
Montague Rd 🔢
YO23 . . . . 27 C3
Montague St
YO23 . . . . 56 B2
Montague Wlk 🔳
YO26 . . . . 16 B2
Montrose Ave
YO31 . . . . 46 C1
Monument Cl
YO24 . . . . 55 A4
Moor Cl YO19 . . . . 30 B1
Moorcroft Rd
YO24 . . . . 59 C4
Moore Ave YO10 . . 53 A1
Moorgarth Ave 🔳
YO24 . . . . 54 C4
Moorgate YO24 . . . 54 C4
Moor Gr YO23 . . . . 55 A1
Moor La
  Bilbrough LS24 . . . . 25 A2
  Bishopthorpe YO23. 26 C4
  Copmanthorpe
  YO23 . . . . 26 C2
  Haxby YO32 . . . . . . 10 C4
  Knapton YO26 . . . . 21 A3
  Murton YO19 . . . . . 17 C1
  Naburn YO19 . . . . . 27 C1
  Newton-on-Ouse
  YO30 . . . . .8 B4
  Rufforth YO26 . . . . 21 A3
  Skelton YO30 . . . . . 39 C3
  Strensall YO32 . . . . 12 A4
  Thornton-le-Clay
  YO60 . . . . .7 B3
  York YO24 . . . . 59 B3
Moorland Garth 🔢
YO32 . . . . 11 C4
Moorland Gdns 🔳
YO23 . . . . 26 C2
Moorland Rd
YO10 . . . . 56 C1
Moorlands YO32 . . 10 A2
Moorlands Cl
YO10 . . . . 53 B1
Moorlands Fields
YO10 . . . . 57 A1
Moorlands La
  Skelton YO30 . . . . . 39 B3
  🔳 Tollerton YO61 . . 2 A4
Moorlands Nature
Reserve✱ YO32 . . 10 A2
Moor Rd YO41 . . . . 19 C1
Moor Way YO32 . . 42 C1
Morcar Rd YO41 . . 19 C2
Morehall Cl YO30 . 45 B3
Morrell Cl
  Woodthorpe
  YO24 . . . . 54 A1
  York YO24 . . . . 54 A1
Morrell Way YO10 57 C3
Morritt Cl 🔳
YO31 . . . . 47 B1
Moss St YO23 . . . . 65 A1
Mount Ephraim 🔳
YO24 . . . . 55 A4
Mount Par YO24 . . 55 C4
Mount Sch The
YO24 . . . . 55 C4
Mount Terr YO24 . . 55 C4
Mount The YO24 . . 65 A1
Mount Vale YO24 . 55 C3
Mount Vale Dr
YO24 . . . . 55 C3
Mowbray Dr YO26 49 B1
Muirfield Way 🔳
YO26 . . . . 49 A2
Mulberry Ct YO32. 42 B3
Mulberry Dr 🔢
YO32 . . . . 11 A2
Mulwith Cl YO31 . . 47 A3
Muncastergate
YO31 . . . . 52 A4
Murray St YO24 . . 55 C4
Murrough Wilson Pl
🔳 YO31 . . . . 64 C4

MURTON 22 C4
Murton La YO19 .. 22 C4
Murton Way YO19 22 B4
Museum St YO1 .. 65 B2
Myrtle Ave YO23 .. 27 C3

N

NABURN 27 C1
Naburn CE Prim Sch
YO19............ 27 C1
Naburn La
Deighton YO19 .... 35 C4
Fulford YO19..... 61 C1
Naburn Park Mews
YO19............ 28 A1
Nairn Cl YO24 .. 59 B3
Nalton Cl 3 YO23 26 C2
Narrow La YO42 .. 38 C4
National Ctr for Early
Music* YO1 .... 65 C2
National Rly Mus*
YO26............ 50 C1
Navigation Rd
YO1............. 65 C2
Nelson's La YO31.. 55 B2
Nelson St YO24.. 64 C4
Nessgate YO1 .. 65 B2
NETHER
POPPLETON ... 16 C2
Nether Way 20
YO26............ 16 B2
Netherwindings 18
YO32............ 11 B2
Netherwoods 5
YO32............. 6 A1
Neville Dr 8
YO23........... 27 C3
Neville St YO31.. 64 C4
Neville Terr YO31 . 64 C4
Nevinson Gr YO10 57 A1
Nevis Way YO24 .. 59 A4
Newborough St
YO30............ 64 A4
Newbury Ave
YO24........... 54 C2
Newby Terr YO31 . 51 B4
Newdale 3 YO32.. 11 B2
NEW EARSWICK . 46 C4
New Earswick Prim
Sch YO32........ 41 C1
New Earswick Sports
Club YO32....... 46 C4
New Forge Ct 19
YO32........... 11 B2
Newgate YO1..... 65 B2
Newgate Ct YO1 .. 65 B2
New La
Bishopthorpe
YO23........... 60 C1
Holgate YO24 ..... 55 A4
Huntington YO32 .. 47 B2
Lillings Ambo YO60..6 B4
Long Marston
YO23........... 25 A4
Stensall YO32 ..... 6 A1
Newland Park Cl
YO10............ 57 C4
Newland Park Dr
YO10............ 57 B4
Newlands Dr
YO26........... 49 A3
Newlands La
YO26........... 16 A1
Newlands Rd
YO23........... 60 B1
New Rd
Appleton Roebuck
YO23........... 33 A2
Beningbrough YO30 .8 B3
Hessay YO26..... 15 B1
Lillings Ambo YO60.. 6 C4
Wheldrake YO19.. 36 B4
New St YO1 ..... 65 B2
Newton House Ct
YO61............. 4 A4
NEWTON-ON-
OUSE........... 8 A3
Newton Pk YO30.. 8 A4
Newton Rd YO26.. 2 A4
Newton Terr YO1.. 65 B1
New Walk Terr
YO10............ 56 C3
Nicholas Gdns
YO10............ 57 B4

Nicholas St YO10 . 57 B4
Nidd Cl YO26...... 44 A1
Nidd Gr YO24..... 55 A1
Nigel Gr 7 YO24 . 55 B3
Nightingale Cl
YO32........... 47 A2
Ninth Ave YO31... 52 B2
Norfolk St YO23 .. 56 B3
Norman Dr YO26 . 49 A3
Norman St 5
YO10............ 57 C4
Norseway 2
YO41........... 19 C2
Northcote Ave
YO24........... 55 A4
Northcroft 5
YO32........... 11 B2
North Eastern Terr
YO24........... 55 A1
North Field Ave
YO23........... 33 B2
North Field Cl
YO23........... 33 B2
North Field La
Askham Bryan
YO23........... 26 B4
Upper Poppleton
YO26........... 21 B4
Northfields 4
YO32............ 6 A1
Northfield Terr
YO24........... 55 A1
North Field Way
YO23........... 33 B2
Northgate La
YO41........... 18 C4
North Grange Ct
YO30........... 64 A4
North La
Dringhouses
YO24........... 55 A1
Huntington YO32.. 42 B2
Wheldrake YO19.. 37 B4
Northlands Ave 1
YO32........... 42 B4
Northminster Bsns
Pk YO30........ 21 B4
North Moor 7
YO32........... 42 B2
Northmoor Cl 8
YO32........... 42 B2
North Moor Gdns
YO32........... 42 B2
North Moor Rd
YO32........... 42 B2
Northolme Dr
YO30........... 45 A2
North Parade
YO30........... 64 A3
North St YO1..... 65 B2
Norway Dr YO10.. 56 C1
Nunmill St YO23 .. 56 B3
Nunnery La YO23 . 65 B1
NUNTHORPE 56 B1
Nunthorpe Ave
YO23........... 56 A3
Nunthorpe Cres
YO23........... 56 A2
Nunthorpe Gr
YO23........... 56 A3
Nunthorpe Rd
YO23........... 65 A1
Nursery Ct
Low Catton YO41 .. 19 B1
Nether Poppleton
YO26........... 16 C2
Nursery Dr YO24.. 55 A4
Nursery Gdns
YO10........... 58 B4
Nursery Rd 4
YO26........... 16 C2

O

Oak Busk La YO60 ..7 B2
Oakdale Rd YO30 . 45 B3
Oak Dr 8 YO32.. 34 B4
Oak Glade 6
YO31........... 47 B4
Oakhill Cres 3
YO32........... 11 C3
Oakland Ave
YO31........... 52 C4
Oakland Dr YO31 . 52 C4
Oaklands 6 YO32 12 A4
Oaklands Sports Ctr
YO24........... 54 B3
Oak Rise 4 YO24. 54 B4

Oak St 3 YO26 .. 50 A2
Oak Tree Cl YO32 . 12 A4
Oak Tree Ct 4
YO32........... 41 C4
Oak Tree Gr YO32. 46 C4
Oak Tree La YO32 . 41 B4
Oak Tree Way 10
YO32........... 12 A4
Oakville St YO31.. 51 C4
Ogleforth YO1.... 64 B3
Old Coppice 14
YO32........... 11 B2
Old Dike Lands 34
YO32........... 11 A1
Old Hall La YO41.. 24 B2
Old Highway The 9
YO32........... 11 B2
Old Lane Ct LS24 . 33 A4
Oldman Ct YO24 . 54 B1
Old Moor La YO24 60 A4
Old Orchard Cl YO32 11 A1
Old Orchard The
Fulford YO10..... 62 A4
Shipton YO30 ..... 9 B2
Old Rd YO23...... 33 A2
Old St The LS24.. 25 B1
Old School Cl
YO19........... 53 A1
Old Village The
YO32........... 42 B2
Olympian Ct YO10 52 B1
OPSA Bsns Ctr
YO1............. 65 B2
Opus Ave YO26 .. 44 B2
Orchard Cl
Appleton Roebuck
YO23........... 33 B2
York YO26....... 55 A2
Orchard Cotts 4
YO19........... 23 B4
Orchard Garth 28
YO23........... 26 C3
Orchard Gdns
YO31........... 47 A3
Orchard Paddock
YO31........... 64 C4
Orchard Rd 6
YO26........... 16 C2
Orchard The
15 Bishopthorpe
YO25........... 27 C3
Heslington YO10.. 57 C2
Orchard View 3
YO30........... 39 A2
Orchard Way
1 Strensall
YO32........... 12 A4
York YO24....... 55 A2
Ordnance La
YO10........... 56 C2
Oriel Gr YO30..... 45 C1
Orrin Cl YO24.... 59 B4
OSBALDWICK... 53 B4
Osbaldwick Ind Est
YO10........... 53 C2
Osbaldwick La
YO10........... 53 B1
Osbaldwick Link Rd
YO10........... 53 B1
Osbaldwick Prim Sch
YO10........... 53 B1
Osbaldwick Village
YO10........... 53 B1
Osbourne Dr 4
YO30........... 45 A4
Osmington Gdns 10
YO32........... 11 C4
Osprey Cl 4
YO24........... 54 A1
Ostler's Cl 9
YO23........... 27 A3
Ostman Rd YO10 . 56 C1
Otterwood Bank 5
YO24........... 54 A2
Otterwood La
YO24........... 54 A2
Otterwood Paddock
YO41........... 19 B1
Our Ladys RC Prim
Sch YO24....... 55 A2
Ouse Acres YO10 . 49 C3
Ouseburn Ave
YO26........... 49 B3
Ousecliffe Gdns
YO30........... 50 C3
Ouse Lea YO30 .. 50 C4
Outgang La YO19 . 53 C3
Overdale Cl YO24. 54 C1

OVERTON 16 B3
Overton Rd YO30 . 16 B4
Ovington Terr
YO23........... 56 A3
Owlwood Cl 7
YO19........... 23 A4
Owlwood La 6
YO19........... 23 A4
Owston Ave 2
YO10........... 57 C4
Ox Calder Cl 16
YO19........... 23 B4
Ox Carr La YO32 .. 12 A4
Ox Cl YO31...... 19 C3
Ox Close La YO10. 22 B1
Oxford St 5 YO24 55 C4

P

Paddock Cl
Askham Richard
YO23........... 25 C4
6 Copmanthorpe
YO23........... 26 C2
Paddocks The
YO19........... 37 C4
Paddock The
YO26........... 49 B3
Paddock Way
YO26........... 49 B3
Palmer La YO1 .. 65 C2
Palmes Cl YO19.. 28 A1
Panman La YO19 . 18 B1
Parade Ct YO31.. 52 B3
Paragon St YO10 . 65 C1
Park Ave YO32 ... 41 C2
Park Cl YO30..... 39 A1
Park Cres YO31... 64 C4
Parker Ave YO26.. 54 A3
Park Est 38 YO32. 11 A1
Park Gate YO32... 6 A1
Park Gr YO31..... 64 C4
Park Grove Prim Sch
YO31........... 64 C4
Park La YO25.... 55 B4
Parkland Way 5
YO32........... 11 A1
Park Lodge YO32 . 41 C1
Park Pl YO31..... 64 C4
Parkside Cl YO24. 55 A4
Parkside Commercial
Ctr YO23....... 65 C1
Park St YO24..... 65 A1
Park Terr YO32 ... 41 C2
Parliament St
YO1............. 65 B2
Parsons La YO26.. 16 A2
Paston Wlk YO23 . 65 B1
Pasture Cl
Skelton YO30 ..... 39 A2
2 Strensall YO32.. 12 A4
Pasture Farm Cl
YO10........... 42 A3
Pasture La YO31.. 48 A1
Pastures The 4
YO24........... 55 A1
Pately Pl 1 YO26. 49 C1
Patrick Pool YO1 . 65 B2
Patterdale Dr
YO30........... 45 A2
Pavement YO1.... 65 B2
Paver La YO1..... 65 C2
Pavilion Row
YO10........... 61 C4
Pear Tree Ave 8
YO26........... 16 B2
Pear Tree Cl YO32. 42 B1
Peartree Ct YO1 . 64 C3
Peasholme Gn
YO1............. 65 C2
Peckitt St YO1... 65 B1
Peel Cl YO10..... 57 C2
Peel St YO1...... 65 C1
Pelham Pl 15
YO10........... 11 C4
Penley's Grove St
YO31........... 64 C4
Pennine Cl YO32.. 42 B1
Penny La Ct YO1.. 64 C3
Pentire Cl 11
YO30........... 45 C2
Pentland Dr YO30. 47 A4
Penyghent Ave
YO31........... 52 C2

Peppercorn Cl 6
YO26........... 50 A1
Percy's La YO1 .. 65 C2
Percy St YO31.... 64 B3
Petercroft Cl 5
YO19........... 23 B4
Petercroft La
YO19........... 23 B4
Peter Hill Dr
YO30........... 45 C1
Peter La YO1..... 65 B2
Petersway YO30.. 64 A3
Pheasant Dr 5
YO24........... 54 A1
Philadelphia Terr 2
YO23........... 56 A3
Phoenix Bvd YO26 50 C1
Picadilly Ct YO1 .. 65 C2
Piccadilly YO1.... 65 C2
Pike Hills Mount 30
YO23........... 26 C3
Piker Thorn La
YO19........... 17 C2
Pilgrim St YO31 .. 64 B4
Pinelands 4
YO32........... 41 C4
Pinelands Way
YO10........... 58 B4
Pinewood Gr 6
YO31........... 47 A3
Pinewood Hill 4
YO10........... 58 B4
Pinfold Ct 4
YO30........... 50 C4
Pinsent Ct 4
YO31........... 47 A1
Pioneer Bsns Pk
YO30........... 45 B4
Plantation Dr
YO26........... 49 B3
Plantation Gr
YO26........... 49 B3
Plantation Way 23
YO32........... 11 A2
Pleasant Ave 3
YO23........... 34 B4
Ploughlands 1
YO32........... 41 B4
Ploughman's Cl 4
YO23........... 27 A3
Ploughmans' La
YO32........... 41 B4
Plumer Ave YO31 . 52 C2
Poplar Gr YO32... 42 A4
Poplar St YO26 .. 56 A2
Poppleton Hall Gdn
YO26........... 16 C3
Poppleton Ousebank
Prim Sch YO26 . 16 B2
Poppleton Rd
YO26........... 50 A1
Poppleton Rd Prim
Sch YO26....... 50 A2
Poppleton Sta
YO26........... 16 B1
Portal Rd
Knapton YO26.... 49 A4
York YO26....... 49 A3
Portisham Pl 12
YO30........... 45 A4
Portland St YO31. 64 B4
Postern Cl YO23.. 65 B1
Postern La YO42.. 38 C3
Potters Dr 8
YO23........... 26 C3
Pottery La
Stensall YO32 ..... 5 C1
York YO31....... 52 A4
Precentor's Ct
YO1............. 64 B3
Prestwick Ct
YO26........... 49 A2
Price's La YO23... 65 B1
Priest La YO19... 23 B2
Princess Dr YO26 . 49 C3
Princess Rd YO32. 12 A4
Prior's Wlk YO26 . 49 C3
Priory St YO1.... 65 A1
Priory Wood Way
YO30........... 51 A4
Prospect Terr
Fulford YO10..... 61 C3
York YO1........ 65 B1
Pulleyn Cl 3 YO32. 42 B1
Pulleyn Dr YO24.. 55 B2
Purey Cust Nuffield
Hospl The YO1.. 64 B3

Q

Quaker Gn 1
YO24........... 59 B4
Quant Mews YO10 58 A4
Queen Annes Rd
YO30........... 64 A3
Queen Margarets
Sch YO19....... 35 C2
Queen's Ct YO1.. 65 B2
Queens Staith Mews
YO1............. 65 B1
Queen's Staith Rd
YO1............. 65 B2
Queen St YO24 .. 65 A2
Queenswood Gr
YO24........... 54 C3
Queen Victoria St
YO23........... 56 A2
Quilt Mus & Gall
The* YO1 ...... 65 C2

R

Racecourse Rd
YO23........... 56 A1
Railway Terr
YO24........... 50 C1
Railway View
YO24........... 55 A1
Rainsborough Way
3 YO30......... 45 C1
Raker Cl YO19.... 37 B4
Ralph Butterfield
Prim Sch YO32 .. 11 B2
Rampart The
YO23........... 32 C1
Ramsay Cl YO31.. 64 C4
Ramsey Ave YO23. 27 C3
Ratcliffe Ct YO30. 39 B2
Ratcliffe St YO30. 51 A4
Raven Gr YO26 .. 49 B1
RAWCLIFFE..... 45 A3
Rawcliffe Ave
YO30........... 45 B1
Rawcliffe Cl 5
YO30........... 45 B1
Rawcliffe Croft
YO30........... 45 A3
Rawcliffe Dr YO30 45 B1
Rawcliffe Ind Est
YO30........... 45 A4
Rawcliffe Infant Sch
YO30........... 45 B2
Rawcliffe La YO30 45 B2
Rawcliffe Landing
YO30........... 38 B4
Rawcliffe Village
YO30........... 45 A4
Rawcliffe Way
YO30........... 45 A3
Rawdon Ave YO10 52 B1
Rectory Cl YO23.. 32 C1
Rectory Gdns
YO23........... 56 A2
Redbarn Dr YO10. 53 C3
Redcap La YO42.. 38 B2
Redcoat Way 1
YO24........... 54 A1
Redeness St YO31 52 A4
Redgrave Cl YO31 47 A1
Redhill Field La
YO23........... 25 C2
Redman Cl YO10.. 56 B3
Redmayne Sq YO32 6 A1
Redmires Cl YO30 45 C3
Redthorn Dr YO31 47 B2
Red Twr* YO1 ... 52 A1
Redwood Dr 6
YO32........... 11 A2
Reeves The YO24. 54 B2
Regency Mews 2
YO24........... 55 B1
Regents Ct 14
YO26........... 49 C1
Regents Mews 1
YO26........... 49 C1
Regent St YO10... 57 A4
Regimental Mus*
YO1............. 65 B1
Reginald Gr YO23. 56 B3
Reid Pk YO32.... 11 A
Reighton Ave
YO30........... 45 A4
Reighton Dr 10
YO30........... 45 B

Renshaw Gdns **8**
YO26 . . . . 50 A1
Retreat Hospl The
YO10 . . . . 57 B3
Reygate Gr **17**
YO23 . . . . 26 C2
Ribstone Gr YO31. 53 A3
Rice La YO60 . . . . . . .7 B3
Richard III Mus*
YO31 . . . . 64 C3
Richardson St
YO23 . . . . 56 B3
Richmond St
YO31 . . . . 52 A2
Ridgeway YO26 . . . 54 A4
Ringstone Rd
Bishopthorpe
YO23 . . . . 61 A1
York YO30 . . . . 45 B4
Ripley Gr **3** YO32. 11 A2
Risewood YO41 . . . 19 A3
Rishworth Gr
YO30 . . . . 45 B3
Rivelin Way YO30 . 45 B3
Riversdale **17**
YO32 . . . . 11 B2
Riverside Cl **1**
YO41 . . . . 31 B3
Riverside Cres
YO32 . . . . 42 B3
Riverside Gdns
2 Elvington
YO41 . . . . 31 B3
2 Poppleton YO26. 16 B2
Riverside Wlk
1 Poppleton
YO26 . . . . 16 B2
5 Strensall YO32. 11 C4
River St YO23 . . . . 65 B1
Riversvale Dr **21**
YO26 . . . . 16 B2
Robert Wilkinson
Prim Sch YO32 . . 11 C4
Robin Gr **6** YO24. 55 B4
Robinson Cl YO1 . 65 C2
Robinson Dr YO24 54 A3
Roche Ave YO31. 47 A1
Rockingham Ave
YO31 . . . . 52 C2
Roecliffe Ct YO26. 15 B1
Rogers Ct
Woodthorpe
YO24 . . . . 54 B1
York YO24 . . . . 54 B1
Roland Ct YO32. 47 A4
Rolston Ave **3**
YO31 . . . . 47 A1
Roman Avenue N **17**
YO41 . . . . 19 C3
Roman Avenue S
YO41 . . . . 19 C2
Ropers Ct **3**
YO23 . . . . 27 A3
Ropewalk The
YO31 . . . . 52 A2
Roseberry Gr
YO30 . . . . 45 B4
Rosebery St YO30. 50 B3
Rosecomb Way **6**
YO32 . . . . 41 C4
Rosecroft Way
YO30 . . . . 45 A1
Rosedale Ave
YO26 . . . . 49 B1
Rosedale St YO10. 56 C4
Rosemary Ct YO1. 65 C2
Rosemary Pl YO1. 65 C2
Rose St YO31 . . . . 51 B4
Rose Tree Gr
YO32 . . . . 41 C1
Rosetta Way YO26 49 C3
Rosslyn St **1**
YO30 . . . . 50 B2
Rougier St YO1 . . 65 A2
Round Hill Link
YO30 . . . . 45 B3
Rowan Ave YO32 . 41 C1
Rowan Pl YO32 . . 41 C1
Rowley Ct **2**
YO32 . . . . 42 B4
Rowmans The
YO30 . . . . 39 B1
Rowntree Ave
YO30 . . . . 46 B1
Royal Chase YO24 55 B1
Ruby St **3** YO23 . 56 A2
Rudcarr La YO19. 18 A2
Ruddings YO19 . . 30 C1

Ruddings Cl **13**
YO23 . . . . 11 A1
Ruddings The
YO19 . . . . 30 C1
Ruffhams Cl YO19 30 B1
RUFFORTH 20 B3
Rufforth Prim Sch
YO23 . . . . 20 B3
Runswick Ave
YO26 . . . . 49 A1
Rushwood Cl **6**
YO32 . . . . 11 B2
Russell Dr YO30 . 45 B3
Russell St YO23 . . 56 A3
Russet Dr YO31 . . 53 A2
Rutland Cl **28**
YO23 . . . . 26 C3
Ryburn Cl YO30. . 45 B3
Rydal Ave YO31 . . 52 C3
Rye Cl **11** YO32 . . 11 A1
Ryecroft **7** YO32 . 11 C3
Ryecroft Ave
YO32 . . . . 59 B4
Ryecroft Cl YO31 . 48 B1
Ryehill Cl YO23 . . 41 C2
Ryemoor Rd **29**
YO32 . . . . 11 A1
Rylatt Pl YO26 . . . 54 A4

S

Sadberge Ct YO10 58 B4
Saddlers Cl
2 Copmanthorpe
YO23 . . . . 26 C3
Huntington YO32 . 47 B3
Saddlers Wlk
YO19 . . . . 35 C2
Sails Dr YO10. . . . 58 A4
St Aelreds Cl
YO31 . . . . 52 B1
St Aelreds RC Prim
Sch YO31 . . . . . . 53 A2
St Andrewgate
YO1 . . . . 65 B2
St Andrew Pl YO1. 65 C2
St Ann Ct YO10 . . 57 A3
St Ann's Ct YO10 . 56 C3
St Aubyn's Pl
YO24 . . . . 55 C3
St Barnabas CE Prim
Sch YO26 . . . . . . 50 B2
St Barnabas Ct **13**
YO26 . . . . 50 B2
St Benedict Rd
YO23 . . . . 65 A1
St Bridget's Ct
YO23 . . . . 65 B1
St Catherines Cl
YO30 . . . . 39 B2
St Catherines Pl
YO24 . . . . 55 C4
St Chads Wharf
YO23 . . . . 56 B1
St Clement's Gr
YO23 . . . . 56 B3
St Denys' Rd YO1. 65 C2
St Edmunds YO41. 19 C3
St Edward's Cl
YO24 . . . . 55 B1
St George's Pl
YO24 . . . . 55 B3
St Georges RC Prim
Sch YO10 . . . . . . 56 C3
St Giles Ct YO31. . 64 B3
St Giles Rd YO30. . 39 A2
St Giles Way **13**
YO23 . . . . 26 C2
St Gregory's Mews
YO1. . . . . 65 A2
St Helen's Rd **5**
YO24 . . . . 55 C3
St Helen's Rise
YO19 . . . . 37 C4
St Helen's Sq YO1 65 B2
St Hildas Mews
YO10 . . . . 53 A1
St James Cl YO30. 45 A4
St James Croft
YO24 . . . . 54 C2
St James Mount
YO23 . . . . 55 C3
St James Pl **5**
YO23 . . . . 54 C2
St John's Cres
YO31 . . . . 64 C4

St John's Rd **9**
YO41 . . . . 19 C3
St John St YO31 . . 64 B3
St Josephs St **9**
YO24 . . . . 54 A2
St Lawrences CE
Prim Sch YO10 . . 57 A4
St Leonard's Pl
YO30 . . . . 64 B3
St Luke's Gr YO30. 51 A4
St Margaret's Terr
YO1. . . . . 52 A1
St Mark's Gr YO30 45 A3
St Martin's La
YO1. . . . . 65 A2
St Mary's YO30 . . 64 A3
St Mary's Abbey*
YO1. . . . . 65 A3
St Marys CE Prim
Sch YO23 . . . . . . 25 C4
St Marys Cl YO42. 38 B2
St Mary's Cl
15 Haxby YO32. . 11 A2
Strensall YO32 . . 11 C4
St Mary's Ct YO23 65 A1
St Mary's Gr YO10 53 B1
St Mary's La YO30 64 A3
St Mary's Mus*
YO1. . . . . 65 B2
St Marys Terr
YO30 . . . . 64 A3
St Mary's Terr
YO30 . . . . 64 A3
St Matthew's Cl **4**
YO19 . . . . 27 C1
St Maurice's Rd
YO31 . . . . 64 C3
St Michaels Ct **10**
YO24 . . . . 54 A2
St Nicholas Ave
YO19 . . . . 62 A1
St Nicholas Cl **29**
YO23 . . . . 26 C3
St Nicholas Cres **28**
YO23 . . . . 26 C3
St Nicholas Croft
YO23 . . . . 26 A4
St Nicholas Fields*
YO10 . . . . 52 B1
St Nicholas Pl **1**
YO10 . . . . 57 B4
St Nicholas Rd **27**
YO10 . . . . 57 B4
St Nicholas Way **22**
YO32 . . . . 11 A2
St Olave's Rd
YO30 . . . . 64 A4
St Olaves Sch
YO30 . . . . 64 A3
St Oswalds CE Prim
Sch YO10 . . . . . . 56 C4
St Oswalds Ct
YO10 . . . . 62 A4
St Oswald's Rd
YO10 . . . . 56 C1
St Pauls CE Prim Sch
YO24 . . . . 55 C4
St Pauls Mews
YO24 . . . . 55 C4
St Paul's Sq YO24. 55 C4
St Paul's Terr
YO24 . . . . 50 C1
St Peters Cl YO26. 21 C4
St Peters Ct YO30. 64 A4
St Peter's Gr
YO30 . . . . 64 A4
St Peters Sch
YO30 . . . . 64 A4
St Philip's Gr
YO30 . . . . 45 C1
St Sampsons Sq
YO1. . . . . 65 B2
St Saviourgate
YO1. . . . . 65 C2
St Saviour's Pl
YO1. . . . . 65 C2
St Stephens Mews
YO24 . . . . 55 C4
St Stephen's Rd
YO24 . . . . 54 A2
St Stephen's Sq
YO24 . . . . 54 B2
St Swithin's Wlk
YO26 . . . . 50 A1
St Thomas' Pl
YO31 . . . . 64 B4
St Thomas's Cl **2**
YO10 . . . . 53 B1

St Wilfreds RC Prim
Sch YO31 . . . . . . 64 C3
St Wilfrid's Cl **7**
YO32 . . . . 12 A3
St Wilfrid's Ct
YO31 . . . . 64 C3
St Wilfrid's Rd **8**
YO32 . . . . 12 A3
St Williams Coll
YO1. . . . . 64 B3
St Wulstan Cl
YO31 . . . . 52 A4
Salisbury Rd YO26 50 B2
Salisbury Ter
YO26 . . . . 50 B2
Salmond Rd **4**
YO24 . . . . 54 A2
Sandacre Ct YO26 49 C2
Sandcroft Cl **4**
YO24 . . . . 54 C1
Sandcroft Rd
YO24 . . . . 54 C1
Sanderson Ct
YO26 . . . . 54 A4
Sandholme **2**
YO32 . . . . 11 B2
SAND HUTTON . . 14 A2
Sand Hutton CE Prim
Sch YO41 . . . . . . 14 A2
Sand Hutton Ct
YO41 . . . . 14 A2
Sandmartin Ct
YO24 . . . . 54 C1
Sandown Cl YO24. 55 A3
Sandringham Cl
YO32 . . . . 41 B4
Sandringham St
YO10 . . . . 56 C3
Sandstock Rd
YO31 . . . . 53 A4
Sandy Gap YO32 . 41 B4
Sandy La
16 Haxby YO32. . 11 A2
Stockton on the Forest
YO32 . . . . 13 A1
Sandyland **25**
YO32 . . . . 11 C2
Sandyridge **9**
YO30 . . . . 45 C1
Sargent Ave YO23. 60 B1
Saville Gr YO30 . . 45 C1
Sawyer's Cres **21**
YO23 . . . . 26 C2
Sawyers Wlk **9**
YO19 . . . . 23 B4
Saxford Way **8**
YO32 . . . . 10 C2
Saxon Cl YO30. . . .9 B2
Saxon Pl YO31 . . . 52 A4
Saxon Rd YO41 . . 19 C3
Saxon Vale YO30. . .9 B2
Scafell Cl **4** YO30 45 A2
Scaggiethorpe La
YO26 . . . . 15 C3
Scaife Gdns YO31. 51 B4
Scaife Mews
YO31 . . . . 51 B4
Scaife St YO31 . . . 51 B4
Scarborough Terr
YO30 . . . . 64 B4
Scarcroft Hill
YO23 . . . . 56 B3
Scarcroft La YO23 65 A1
Scarcroft Prim Sch
YO23 . . . . 56 B3
Scarcroft Rd
YO24 . . . . 65 A1
Scarcroft View
YO23 . . . . 65 B1
Scaudercroft **13**
YO19 . . . . 23 B4
Scawton Ave **1**
YO31 . . . . 47 A1
School Cl **16** YO41 19 C3
School La
Askham Richard
YO23 . . . . 25 C4
Bishopthorpe YO23. 60 C1
Copmanthorpe
YO23 . . . . 26 C2
Heslington YO10 . 53 C3
23 Poppleton YO26. 16 B2
York YO10 . . . . 62 A4
School St YO24 . . 54 C4
Scoreby La
Gate Helmsley
YO41 . . . . 19 A3
Kexby YO41. . . . . . 19 A1
Low Catton YO41 . . 19 A1

Scotchman La
YO60 . . . . 7 C1
Scott Moncrieff Rd
YO32 . . . . 12 A3
Scott St YO23 . . . . 56 B3
Scriven Gr **8**
YO32 . . . . 11 B2
Scrope Ave **4**
YO31 . . . . 52 A2
Seafire Cl YO30. . . 45 C4
Seakel La YO23 . . 25 B3
Seaton Cl YO10 . . 53 B1
Second Ave YO31. 52 B2
Sefton Ave YO31 . 47 B1
Segrave Wlk **10**
YO26 . . . . 50 A1
Selby Rd YO19 . . . 62 A3
Seldon Rd YO26 . . 50 A2
Seventh Ave YO31 52 B2
Severn Gn YO26 . . 44 B1
Severus Ave YO24 49 C1
Severus St YO24 . 54 C4
Seymour Gr YO31. 52 B3
Shallowdale Gr **1**
YO10 . . . . 58 B4
Shaw's Terr YO24. 65 A1
Shelley Gr YO30 . . 45 B2
Sherringham Dr
YO24 . . . . 54 C1
Sherwood Gr
Huntington YO32. . 47 B2
York YO26 . . . . . . 49 A3
Shilton Garth Cl **3**
YO32 . . . . 42 B4
SHIPTON 9 B2
Shipton Low Rd
YO30 . . . . 9 A2
Shipton Rd
Clifton YO30 . . . . 45 B1
Rawcliffe YO30 . . 44 C3
York YO30 . . . . . . 50 C4
Shipton St **3**
YO30 . . . . 51 A4
Shirbutt La YO26 . 15 B1
Shirley Ave YO26 . 49 B3
Short La YO23 . . . 33 C1
Shotel Cl YO30 . . 45 B1
Sidings The YO32. 12 A4
Sills La YO30 . . . . . 8 A3
Silverdale Ct
YO24 . . . . 59 C4
Silver St YO1 . . . . 65 B2
Sim Balk La YO23. 60 A2
Sirocco Ct YO31 . . 46 C1
Sitwell St YO26. . . 49 B2
Siwards Howe*
YO10 . . . . 58 A2
Siward St YO10 . . 57 C4
Siward's Way
YO10 . . . . 57 C3
Sixth Ave YO31 . . 52 A2
Skates La YO61 . . 4 A4
Skeldergate YO1. . 65 B2
SKELTON 39 B3
Skelton Ct **3**
YO30 . . . . 50 B2
Skelton La YO32 . 10 A1
Skelton Park Trading
Est YO30 . . . . . . 39 A1
Skelton Prim Sch
YO30 . . . . 39 B2
Skewsby Gr YO31. 47 B2
Skiddaw YO24 . . . 59 B4
Skipwith Rd YO19. 36 A3
Slessor Rd YO24 . 54 A2
Slingsby Gr YO24 . 55 A1
Smales' St YO1 . . 65 B1
Smeaton Gr YO26. 49 B2
Smeaton Rd YO41 24 C4
Smith Cl YO10 . . 57 B1
Smithie Cl YO32 . 41 C2
Smith's La YO60 . . 6 C2
Snowdon Cl YO23 25 C4
Somerset Cl **6**
YO30 . . . . 45 A4
Somerset Rd
YO31 . . . . 46 C1
South Back La
YO61. . . . . 4 A4
SOUTH BANK . . . 55 C2
South Bank Ave
YO23 . . . . 56 A2
South Down Rd **3**
YO32 . . . . 42 B2
South Esplande
YO1. . . . . 65 B2
Southfield Cl
YO23 . . . . 20 C3

Southfield Cres **2**
YO24 . . . . 55 A1
Southfield Grange **3**
YO23 . . . . 33 B2
Southfields Rd
YO32 . . . . 12 A4
Southlands **4**
YO32 . . . . 11 A2
Southlands Cl
YO19 . . . . 36 A3
Southlands Rd
YO23 . . . . 56 A3
Southmoor Rd
YO19 . . . . 37 B2
Southolme Dr **7**
YO30 . . . . 45 B2
South Parade
YO23 . . . . 65 A1
South Ruddings La
YO19 . . . . 37 B4
Southwood Rd
YO41 . . . . 31 B1
Sowerby Rd YO26. 49 C1
Spalding Ave
YO30 . . . . 51 A4
Speculation St
YO1. . . . . 52 A1
Spencer St **3**
YO23 . . . . 65 B1
Speng La YO23 . . 20 A1
Spen La YO1. . . . . 64 C3
Spey Bank YO24 . 59 B3
Spindle Cl YO24 . . 59 B3
Spinney The YO24. 60 B4
Springbank Ave
YO19 . . . . 23 A4
Springfield Cl
YO31 . . . . 53 A4
Springfield Rd **4**
YO26 . . . . 16 B2
Springfield Way
YO31 . . . . 53 A4
Spring La YO10 . . 57 C2
Springwood YO32 41 C4
Springwood Gr
YO26 . . . . 49 B3
Spruce Cl YO32 . . 46 C3
Spurr Ct YO24 . . . 54 B1
Spurriergate YO1. 65 B2
Stabler Cl **15**
YO32 . . . . 10 C2
Stablers Wlk
YO32 . . . . 42 B4
Staindale Cl YO30 45 A3
Staithes Cl **4**
YO26 . . . . 49 A1
Stamford Bridge
Prim Sch YO41 . . 19 C3
Stamford Bridge Rd
YO19 . . . . 23 A4
Stamford Bridge W
YO41 . . . . 19 B3
Stamford Street E **10**
YO26 . . . . 50 B2
Stamford Street W
8 YO26 . . . . 50 B2
Stanley Ave YO31. 64 B4
Stanley St YO31 . . 64 C4
Starkey Cres
YO31 . . . . 52 C2
Station Ave
New Earswick
YO32 . . . . 46 C4
York YO1. . . . . 65 A2
Station Bsns Pk
YO26 . . . . 50 B1
Station La YO30 . . 9 A2
Station Rd
Copmanthorpe
YO23 . . . . 26 C2
Haxby YO32. . . . . 11 B2
24 Poppleton YO26. 16 B2
Tollerton YO61. . . 2 A4
York YO24 . . . . 54 C4
Station Rise YO1. . 65 B2
Station Sq **4**
YO32 . . . . 12 A4
Steeple Cl **1**
YO23 . . . . 10 C2
Steeton La LS24. . 32 C4
Stephenson Cl
YO31 . . . . 47 A2
Stephenson Way
YO26 . . . . 50 B2
Sterling Pk YO30 . 45 C4

Sterne Ave YO31 . . 52 C2
Sterne Way YO61 . . .4 B4
Stewart La YO19 . . 34 B1
Stirling Gr YO10 . . 57 B1
Stirling Rd YO30 . . 45 B4
Stirrup Cl YO24 . . 54 A1
Stockhill Cl **1**
  YO19 . . . . 23 A4
Stockholm Cl **1**
  YO10 . . . . 56 C1
Stockton Hall Hospl
  YO32 . . . . 17 C4
Stockton La
  Heworth YO32 . . . . 48 C2
  York YO31 . . . . 52 C4
STOCKTON ON THE
  FOREST 17 C4
Stockton on the
  Forest Prim Sch
  YO32 . . . . 17 C4
Stonebow The
  YO1 . . . . 65 C2
Stonegate YO1 . . 64 B3
Stonelands Ct **2**
  YO30 . . . . 45 C2
Stone Riggs YO32. 17 C3
Stones Cl YO24 . . . 55 A3
Stonethwaite **5**
  YO24 . . . . 55 B4
Stonewall Cottage La
  25 YO41 . . . . 19 C3
Stoop Cl **25** YO32 . 11 A1
Stow Ct YO32 . . . . 47 A4
Straight La YO19. . 18 B1
Stratford Way
  YO32 . . . . 47 A4
Stray Garth YO31 . 52 B4
Straylands Gr
  YO31 . . . . 47 B1
Stray Rd YO31 . . . 53 A3
STREET HOUSES 25 B1
Street La LS24 . . . . 32 C4
STRENSALL 11 C4
STRENSALL
  CAMP 12 A3
Strensall Comm
  Nature Reserve*
  YO60 . . . . 6 C1
Strensall Pk YO32. 11 C2
Strensall Rd
  Earswick YO32 . . . . 42 C4
  York YO32 . . . . 42 B3
Stripe La YO30. . . . 39 A2
Stuart Cl **4** YO32. . .6 B1
Stuart Rd YO24 . . . 54 C2
Stubden Gr YO30 . 45 B3
Sturdee Gr YO31. . 51 C4
Summerfield Rd
  YO24 . . . . 59 B4
Summer Gdns
  YO30 . . . . 45 B1
Sunningdale Cl
  Knapton YO26. . . . . 49 A2
  1 York YO26 . . . . . 49 A2
Sunnydale **3**
  YO32 . . . . 41 C4
Surrey Way YO30 . 45 B1
Surtees St YO30 . . 51 A4
Sussex Cl YO10 . . 58 B3
Sussex Rd YO10 . . 58 B3
Sussex Way **14**
  YO32 . . . . 11 C4
Sutherland St
  YO23 . . . . 56 A2
Sutor Cl **19** YO23. 26 C3
Sutton Bridge*
  YO41 . . . . 31 B3
SUTTON-ON-THE-
  FOREST 4 B4
Sutton-on-the-
  Forest CE Prim Sch
  YO61. . . . . .4 B4
Sutton Pk* YO61 . . .4 B4
Sutton Rd YO32 . . 10 C4
SUTTON UPON
  DERWENT 31 B2
Sutton upon Derwent
  CE Prim Sch
  YO41 . . . . 31 B3
Sutton Way YO30 . 45 B1
Swale Ave YO24 . . 55 A1
Swan Cl YO19 . . . 35 C4
Swan Farm Ct
  YO19 . . . . 35 C4
Swann St YO23 . . 65 A1
Swinegate YO1 . . 65 B2

Swinegate Court E
  YO1 . . . . 64 B3
Swinsty Ct YO30 . 45 B2
Swinton Cl **8**
  YO30 . . . . 45 A3
Sycamore Ave
  YO32 . . . . 41 C1
Sycamore Cl
  1 Haxby YO32 . . . 41 C4
  Skelton YO30 . . . . . 39 B2
Sycamore Pl
  New Earswick
  YO32 . . . . 41 C4
  York YO30 . . . . 64 A3
Sycamore Terr
  YO30 . . . . 64 A3
Sycamore View **17**
  YO26 . . . . 16 B2
Sykes La YO61. . . . . 2 A4

T

Tadcaster Rd **34**
  YO24 . . . . 26 C3
Tadcaster Rd
  Dringhouses
  YO23 . . . . 60 A2
Tamworth Rd **9**
  YO30 . . . . 45 C2
TANG HALL 52 B2
Tang Hall La
  YO31 . . . . 52 C2
Tang Hall Prim Sch
  YO31 . . . . 52 C2
Tanner Row YO1. . 65 A2
Tanner's Moat
  YO1 . . . . 65 A2
Tanner St YO1 . . . 65 B2
Tannery The **10**
  YO10 . . . . 57 A4
Tarbert Cres **2**
  YO24 . . . . 59 A4
Tatton Cl YO30. . . 45 C2
Taurus Ct YO31 . . 65 A1
Teal Dr YO24 . . . . 54 B1
Tedder Rd YO24 . . 54 A2
Telford Terr **1**
  YO24 . . . . 56 A3
Temple Ave YO10 . 53 A1
Temple Garth
  YO23 . . . . 27 A2
Temple La YO23 . . 27 A1
Templemead
  YO31 . . . . 47 A1
Temple Rd YO23 . . 60 B1
Tennent Rd YO24 . 54 A3
Tennyson Ave
  YO30 . . . . 51 B4
Ten Thorn La
  YO26 . . . . 21 C3
Terrington Ct YO32. 6 A1
Terry Ave YO1 . . . 65 B1
Terry St YO23 . . . 56 B2
Thanet Rd YO24 . . 54 C2
Thatchers Croft **33**
  YO23 . . . . 26 C3
Theresa Cl **6**
  YO31 . . . . 47 B2
Thief La YO10 . . . 57 B4
Third Ave YO31 . . 52 B2
Thirkleby Walk
  YO10 . . . . 58 C4
Thirkleby Way
  YO10 . . . . 53 B1
Thirlmere Dr
  YO31 . . . . 52 C3
Thomas St **2**
  YO10 . . . . 57 A4
Thompson Dr **2**
  YO30 . . . . 6 A1
Thompson Pl **6**
  YO26 . . . . 50 A2
Thoresby Rd
  YO26 . . . . 54 A2
THORGANBY 38 A1
Thornbeck YO19. . 23 A3
Thorncroft **8**
  YO19 . . . . 23 B4
Thornfield Ave **5**
  YO31 . . . . 47 B1
Thornfield Dr **7**
  YO31 . . . . 47 A3
Thornhills **19**
  YO32 . . . . 11 B2
Thorn Nook YO31. 47 B1
Thornton Moor Cl
  YO30 . . . . 45 B3

Thorntree Gr
  YO30 . . . . 46 A3
Thornwood Covert **1**
  YO24 . . . . 54 B2
Thorpe St YO23 . . 56 A3
Tilmire Cl **2**
  YO10 . . . . 57 B1
Tinker La YO23 . . 20 C3
Tithe Cl YO24. . . . 54 A2
Toby Ct YO32 . . . 11 C4
Toft Gn YO1 . . . . 65 A2
Tollerton La YO30.. 8 A4
Top La YO23 . . . . 26 C3
Toremill Cl YO32. . 41 C1
Torridon Pl YO24 . 59 A4
Tostig Ave YO26 . 49 B2
Tostig Cl **14** YO41 . 19 C3
Tower Cl YO30. . . 45 C3
Tower Pl YO1 . . . 65 B1
Tower St YO1 . . . 65 B1
Town End Gdns **3**
  YO32 . . . . 10 C2
Townend St YO31. 64 B4
TOWTHORPE . . . 12 A2
Towthorpe Moor La
  YO32 . . . . 12 B2
Towthorpe Rd
  YO32 . . . . 11 B2
Towton Ave **1**
  YO24 . . . . 55 C3
Trafalgar St YO23. 56 A2
Tranby Ave YO10.. 53 C1
Trenchard Rd
  YO26 . . . . 49 A3
Trenfield Ct YO24 . 55 B4
Trent Ave **4** YO32 42 B3
Trentholme Dr **2**
  YO24 . . . . 56 B1
Trent Way YO24 . . 59 C4
Trevor Gr **8** YO24 55 B3
Tribune Way
  YO30 . . . . 46 A3
Trinity La YO1 . . . 65 A2
Trinity Mdws
  YO30 . . . . 17 C4
Troon Cl **2** YO26 . 49 A2
Troutbeck **7**
  YO24 . . . . 59 B4
Troutsdale Ave
  YO30 . . . . 45 A3
Tudor Rd YO24 . . 54 C2
Tudor Way YO32. . .6 B1
Tuke Ave YO10. . . 53 A1
Turbary La YO32 . 17 B4
Turks Head Ct
  YO1. . . . . 64 C3
Turnberry Dr
  YO26. . . . . 49 A1
Turner's Croft
  YO10 . . . . 57 C2
Turnmire Rd **1**
  YO24 . . . . 55 A1
Turpin Ct YO1 . . . 65 C1
Twin Pike Way **14**
  YO32 . . . . 10 C2
Tyn Garth YO19 . . 27 C1

U

Ullswater YO24 . . 59 C4
Undercroft **7**
  YO19. . . . . 23 B4
Union Terr YO31 . . 64 B4
University of York
  (King's Manor)
  YO30 . . . . 64 A3
University of York
  (Main Campus)
  YO10 . . . . 57 C2
University Rd
  YO10 . . . . 57 B3
Uppercroft **4**
  YO32 . . . . 11 A1
Upper Hanover St **6**
  YO26 . . . . 50 B2
UPPER
  HELMSLEY 19 A4
Upper Newborough
  St **1** YO30. . . . . . 51 B4
UPPER
  POPPLETON . . . 16 B2
Upper Price St
  YO23 . . . . 65 A1
Upper St Paul's Terr
  YO24 . . . . 50 C1
Usher La YO32. . . 11 B3

Vale The YO30 . . . 39 A2
Valley View YO19. 37 B4
Vanbrugh Dr
  YO10 . . . . 58 B4
Vanbrugh Way
  YO10 . . . . 57 C3
Vavasour Ct **13**
  YO23 . . . . 26 C2
Vernon Cl **5**
  YO23 . . . . 27 C3
Vernon Rd YO30 . 45 A3
Vesper Dr YO24. . 54 A4
Vesper Wlk YO24. 42 B3
Vicarage Gdns **1**
  YO10 . . . . 53 B1
Vicarage La YO19. 28 A1
Vicars Cl **16** YO23. 26 C2
Victoria **15**
  YO26 . . . . 50 B2
Victoria Farm Cl
  YO23 . . . . 20 B3
Victoria St **1**
  YO23 . . . . 65 B1
Victoria Way **2**
  YO32 . . . . 47 B1
Victor St YO1. . . . 65 B1
Viking Cl **20** YO41. 19 C3
Viking Rd
  Stamford Bridge
  YO41 . . . . 19 C3
  York YO26 . . . . 49 B2
Villa Ct YO26 . . . 49 A4
Village Garth **1**
  YO32 . . . . 11 A2
Village St YO30 . . 45 A4
Village The
  Haxby YO32. . . . . . 11 A2
  Skelton YO30 . . . . . 39 A2
  Stockton on the Forest
  YO32 . . . . 18 A4
  Strensall YO32 . . . . 12 A4
  York YO10. . . . . . . 53 B1
Villa Gr **2** YO31 . 52 A3
Vincent Way YO24 54 B1
Vine St YO23 . . . 56 B3
Vyner St YO31 . . 51 B4

W

Waggoners Dr **7**
  YO23 . . . . 26 C3
Waincroft **8**
  YO32 . . . . 11 C3
Wainers Cl **9**
  YO23 . . . . 26 C3
Wain's Gr YO24. . 59 C4
Wain's Rd YO24. . 54 C1
Walker Dr YO24. . 54 B1
Walker La YO19. . 37 B4
Walkington La
  YO30 . . . . 2 A1
Walmer Carr
  Haxby YO32. . . . . . 10 C2
  Wigginton YO32 . . . 10 C2
Walmgate YO1 . . 65 C2
WALMGATE
  STRAY 57 B2
Walney Rd YO31. 52 C2
Walnut Cl
  39 Haxby YO32. . . 11 A2
  39 Wigginton YO32. 11 A2
  York YO10. . . . . . . 57 C2
Walpole St YO31. 51 C4
Waltham Cl YO32 . .6 A1
Walton Pl YO31. . 52 A2
Walworth Street N **4**
  YO26 . . . . 56 B3
Walworth Street S **9**
  YO26 . . . . 50 B2
Wandhill **31** YO32. 11 A2
Wandle The YO26. 21 C2
Wansbeck **3**
  YO24 . . . . 59 A4
Ward Ct YO23 . . . 65 B1
Warehill La YO61 . . 2 B3
WARTHILL 18 B3
Warthill CE Prim Sch
  YO19. . . . . 18 B3
Warwick St YO31. 51 C4
Wasdale Cl **2**
  YO30 . . . . 45 A2
Waterdale Pk
  YO31 . . . . 47 A2
Water End YO26 . 50 A2

Waterings **19**
  YO32 . . . . 10 C2
Water La
  8 Clifton YO30 . . . 45 C2
  Dunnington YO19 . . 23 B4
  York YO30 . . . . 50 C4
Waterline Ind Est
  YO23 . . . . 34 A4
Waterman Ct **3**
  YO24 . . . . 54 A2
Waterside Gdns
  YO31 . . . . 46 C1
Wath La YO41 . . . 19 B1
Watson St YO24 . 55 C4
Watson Terr **2**
  YO24 . . . . 55 C4
Wattlers Cl **2**
  YO23 . . . . 27 A3
Waveney Gr YO30. 46 A1
Waverley St YO31. 64 C3
Waynefleet Gr **3**
  YO10 . . . . 57 C4
Weavers Cl **14**
  YO23 . . . . 27 C3
Weavers Pk **13**
  YO23 . . . . 26 C3
Weddall Cl YO24. 55 B2
Welborn Cl YO10 . 52 C1
Welland Rise
  YO26 . . . . 49 C2
Wellesley Cl YO30 45 C3
Wellington Row
  YO1. . . . . 65 A2
Wellington St
  YO10 . . . . 57 A4
Welton Ave YO24 . 49 C2
Welwyn Dr YO10. . 57 A1
Wenham Rd YO24. 54 B1
Wenlock Dr YO19 . 36 A3
Wenlock Terr
  YO10 . . . . 56 C2
Wensleydale Dr
  YO10 . . . . 53 C1
Wentworth Rd
  YO24 . . . . 56 A3
Wentworth Way
  YO10 . . . . 57 B3
Werkdyke The
  YO1. . . . . 64 C3
Wesley Pl YO1. . . 65 C2
West Bank YO24 . 55 A4
West End YO32 . . 11 C4
West End Ave
  YO23 . . . . 33 B2
West End Cl **9**
  YO32 . . . . 12 A4
Westerdale Ct **2**
  YO30 . . . . 50 C3
Western Terr
  YO32 . . . . 46 C4
WEST FIELD . . . 21 C2
Westfield Cl **21**
  YO32 . . . . 11 A2
Westfield Ct **10**
  YO23 . . . . 26 C2
Westfield Dr
  YO10 . . . . 56 C1
Westfield Gr **12**
  YO32 . . . . 10 C2
Westfield La
  Thorganby YO19. . . 37 C2
  Wigginton YO32 . . . 10 C2
West Field La
  YO26 . . . . 16 A2
Westfield Pl
  19 Haxby YO32. . . 11 A2
  York YO24 . . . . 54 A3
Westfield Prim Com
  Sch YO24 . . . . 54 A3
Westfield Rd **20**
  YO32 . . . . 11 A2
Westholme Dr
  YO30 . . . . 44 C3
Westlands Gr
  YO31 . . . . 52 B4
Westminster Bsns
  Ctr YO26. . . . . 44 B1
Westminster Pl
  YO26 . . . . 44 A2
Westminster Rd
  YO30 . . . . 50 C3
West Moor La
  YO23 . . . . 58 A1
West Nooks **26**
  YO32 . . . . 11 B2
Westpit La YO32 . 11 C4
West Thorpe
  YO24 . . . . 54 C1
Westview Cl YO26 49 A4

West Wood La
  YO23 . . . . 21 A1
Westwood Mews **12**
  YO19 . . . . 23 B4
Westwood Terr
  YO23 . . . . 56 A2
Wetherby Rd
  YO26 . . . . 54 A4
Wharfe Dr YO24 . 54 C1
Wharncliffe Dr
  YO30 . . . . 45 B3
Wharton Ave
  YO30 . . . . 51 A4
Wharton Rd **8**
  YO41 . . . . 19 C3
Wheatcroft **6**
  YO32 . . . . 11 C3
Wheatfield La
  YO32 . . . . 11 A1
Wheatlands Gr
  YO26 . . . . 49 B3
Wheatley Dr **17**
  YO32 . . . . 11 A1
Wheelhouse The **4**
  YO30 . . . . 39 A2
Wheelwright Cl
  YO41 . . . . 31 B2
Wheel Wright Cl **32**
  YO23 . . . . 26 C3
WHELDRAKE . . . 37 C4
Wheldrake CE Prim
  Sch YO19 . . . . 30 C1
Wheldrake Ings
  Nature Reserve*
  YO19 . . . . 38 B4
Wheldrake La
  YO19 . . . . 36 A2
Whenby Gr YO31 . 47 B2
Whernside Ave
  YO31. . . . . 52 C2
Whin Cl
  3 Strensall
  YO32 . . . . 12 A3
  York YO24 . . . . 60 B4
Whin Garth YO24. 60 B3
Whinny La YO60 . 13 C4
Whin Rd YO24 . . 60 B3
Whip-ma-whop-ma-
  gate YO1 . . . . 65 C2
Whistler Cl **6**
  YO23 . . . . 27 A3
Whitby Ave YO31 . 52 C4
Whitby Dr YO31. . 52 C4
Whitecross Gdns
  YO31 . . . . 51 C4
White Cross Rd
  YO31 . . . . 51 C4
White Horse Cl **6**
  YO32 . . . . 42 B2
White House Dale
  YO24 . . . . 55 B2
White House Dr
  YO24 . . . . 55 B2
White House Gdns **4**
  YO24 . . . . 55 C3
White House Gr **1**
  YO41 . . . . 31 B3
White House Rise
  YO24 . . . . 55 B2
White Rose Ave **3**
  YO32 . . . . 46 C4
White Rose Cl
  YO26 . . . . 44 B2
Whiterose Dr
  YO41 . . . . 19 C1
White Rose Gr **5**
  YO32 . . . . 46 C4
White Rose Way
  YO24 . . . . 44 B2
Whitestone Dr
  YO31 . . . . 47 A
Whitethorn Cl
  YO31 . . . . 47 A
Whitley Cl YO30 . 45 C
Whitley Rd YO41.. 30 C
Whitton Pl YO31 . 53 B
WIGGINTON . . . . 10 C
Wigginton Prim Sch
  YO32 . . . . 10 C
Wigginton Rd
  YO31 . . . . 64 B
Wigginton Terr
  YO31 . . . . 46 B
Wilberforce Ave
  YO30 . . . . 51 A
Wilkinson Way **3**
  YO32 . . . . 11 C
Willans Gr YO26 . 50 A
William Ct YO10 . 57 A

William Plows Ave YO10 . . . . 57 A3
Willis St YO10 . . . 57 A4
Willoughby Way YO24 . . . . 54 A1
Willow Bank YO32 . . . . 42 A1
Willow Ct YO41 . . 19 B3
Willow Glade YO32 . . . . 47 B4
Willow Gr
　Earswick YO32 . . 42 C4
　York YO31 . . . . 52 B4
Willows The
　7 Acaster Malbis YO32 . . . . 34 B4
　8 Strensall YO32 . 12 A4
Wilsthorpe Gr 1 YO10 . . . . 57 B1
Wilstrop Farm Rd 8 YO23 . . . . 26 C2
Wilton Rise YO24 . 55 B4
Wimpole Cl 6 YO30 . . . . 45 C2
Winchester Ave 3 YO26 . . . . 50 A1
Winchester Gr 1 YO26 . . . . 50 A1
Windermere YO24 . . . . 59 C4
Windmill La YO10. 58 A3
Windmill Rise YO26 . . . . 55 A4

Windmill Way 23 YO32 . . . . 11 B2
Windsor Dr 2 YO32 . . . . 10 C2
Windsor Garth YO24 . . . . 54 C2
Windsor St 1 YO23 . . . . 56 A2
Winscar Gr 9 YO30 . . . . 45 A4
Winterscale Ct TO1. . . . . 56 C3
Winterscale St YO10. . . . 56 C3
Witham Dr YO32. . 42 C3
Woburn Cl YO33. . 6 A1
Woldcroft YO41. . 31 B3
Wolfe Ave YO31. . 52 B2
Wolsey Dr 6 YO23 . . . . 27 C3
Wolsley St YO10 . 57 A4
Wolviston Ave YO10 . . . . 65 B2
Wood Cl 7 YO32 . 11 C4
Woodcock Cl 9 YO32 . . . . 11 B2
Woodford Pl 1 YO24 . . . . 54 C2
Woodhouse Gr 4 YO31 . . . . 52 C2
Woodland Chase YO30 . . . . 46 A2

Woodland Pl YO32 . . . . 42 A1
Woodlands YO19 . 36 A2
Woodlands Ave 19 YO32 . . . . 11 A1
Woodlands Gr YO31 . . . . 52 C4
Woodland Way YO32 . . . . 42 B1
Woodlea Ave YO26 . . . . 49 B1
Woodlea Bank YO26 . . . . 49 C1
Woodlea Cres YO26 . . . . 49 C1
Woodlea Gr YO26. 49 C2
Woodleigh Cl 2 YO32 . . . . 11 C3
Woodside Ave YO31 . . . . 52 C3
Woodsmill Quay YO1. . . . . 65 B2
Wood St YO31. . . 52 A2
WOODTHORPE . . 59 B4
Woodthorpe Prim Sch YO24 . . . 59 B4
Wood Way YO32 . 42 C1
Woolnough Ave YO10. . . . . 58 A4
Worcester Dr YO31. . . . . 53 A2
Wordsworth Cres YO24 . . . . 59 C4

Wray's Ave YO31. . 47 A2
Wycliffe Ave YO10. . . . . 58 A4
Wydale Rd YO10 . 53 C1
Wykeham Rd YO26 . . . . 21 B4
Wynam La YO41 . 31 B2

Y
Yarburgh Gr 2 YO26 . . . . 50 A2
Yarburgh Way YO10. . . . . 58 B4
Yearsley Cres YO31. . . . . 51 C4
Yearsley Gr YO31 . 47 A2
Yearsley Grove Prim Sch YO31. . . 47 B2
Yearsley Swimming Pool YO31 . . . 46 C1
Yew Tree Cl
　Acaster Malbis YO23 . . . . 27 B1
　Rufforth YO23. . 20 B3
Yew Tree Mews YO19. . . . . 53 B2
YMR Exhibition* YO10. . . . . 65 A2
YORK. 64 B3
York Barbican Ctr YO10. . . . . 65 C1

York Brewery* YO1. . . . . 65 A2
York Bridge Rd YO61. . . . . 2 A3
York Castle Mus* YO1. . . . . 65 C1
York Coll YO24 . . 60 A3
York Designer Outlet YO19. . . . . 61 C1
York Dungeon The* YO1. . . . . 65 B2
York Eco Bsns Ctr YO30. . . . . 45 C4
York High Sch YO24 . . . . 54 B3
York Hospl YO30. . 64 B4
York La YO60 . . . 7 A1
York Maze* YO19. 23 B1
York Minster* YO1. . . . . 64 B3
York Racecourse (The Knavesmire)* YO24 . . . . 55 C2
York Rd
　Bilbrough YO23. . 25 A3
　Dunnington YO19 . 22 C3
　Haxby YO32. . . . 41 C4
　Naburn YO19. . . 27 C1
　Stillingfleet YO19 . 34 C1
　Strensall YO32 . . 11 C3
　Sutton-on-the-Forest YO61. . . . . 4 B1
　York YO26 . . . . 54 B4

York St John University (Lord Major's Walk Main Campus) YO31. . 64 B3
York Science Park YO10. . . . . 58 A3
Yorkshire Air Mus* YO41. . . . . 30 B4
Yorkshire Mus* YO30. . . . . 64 A3
Yorkshire Mus of Farming* YO19. . 22 B4
York St 5 YO19 . . 23 A4
York Sta YO24 . . 65 A2
York Steiner Sch YO10. . . . . 56 C2
York Theatre Royal* YO1. . . . . 64 B3

Numbered locations

In some busy areas of the maps it is not always possible to show the name of every place. Where not all names will fit, some smaller places are shown by a number. If you wish to find out the name associated with a number, use this listing. *The places in this list are also listed normally in the Index.*

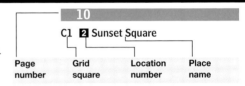

10
C1 2 Sunset Square

| Page number | Grid square | Location number | Place name |

2
A4 1 Moorlands La
2 Green The
3 Kyle Cl
4 Hambleton View
5 Church Cl
6 Jubilee Ct

6
A1 1 Lakeside Gr
2 Thompson Dr
3 Blacklee Cl
4 Northfields
5 Netherwoods
6 Littlethorpe Cl
B1 1 Chapman Cl
2 Brunswick Cl
3 Pulleyn Cl
4 Stuart Cl
5 Coulson Cl
6 Cundall Cl

10
C2 1 Castle Cl
2 Windsor Dr
3 Town End Gdns
4 Steeple Cl
5 Harewood Cl
6 Delamere Cl
7 Eton Dr
8 Saxford Way
9 Canterbury Cl
10 Hambleton View
11 Back La
12 Westfield Gr
13 Burrill Dr
14 Twin Pike Way
15 Stabler Cl
16 Helmsley Gr
17 Corner Cl
18 Lancar Cl
19 Waterings
20 Butters Cl
21 Corban Way
22 Butt Hill

11
A1 1 Lockey Croft
2 Minster View
3 Minster Cl
4 Uppercroft
5 Parkland Way
6 Orchard Paddock
7 Cherry Orch
8 Dealtry Ave
9 Kirkcroft
10 Arenhall Cl
11 Rye Cl
12 Heslin La
13 Ruddings Cl
14 Bell Cl
15 Chestnuts The
16 Barley View
17 Wheatley Dr
18 Becks Cl
19 Woodlands Ave
20 Copwood Gr
21 Meadow La
22 Cherry Paddock
23 Green Dike
24 Lund Cl
25 Stoop Cl
26 Mancroft
27 Hunters Cl
28 Long Furrow
29 Ryemoor Rd
30 Cornwood Way
31 Little Mdws
32 Avenue The
33 Holly Tree La
34 Old Dale Lands
35 Jubilee Ct
36 Park Est
37 Greenshaw Dr
A2 1 Village Garth
2 Longcroft
3 Ripley Gr
4 Southlands
5 Avenue The
6 Redwood Dr
7 Mulberry Dr
8 Ash La
9 Elm End
10 Coppice Cl
11 Little La
12 Hawthorne Ave
13 Birch La
14 Fletcher Ct
15 St Mary's Cl
16 Sandy La
17 Church La
18 Broad Oak La
19 Westfield Pl
20 Westfield Rd
21 Westfield Cl
22 St Nicholas Way
23 Plantation Way
24 Middle Banks
25 Hornsey Garth
26 Glebe Way
27 Forest Cl
28 Churchfield Dr
29 Sandyland
30 Headland Cl
31 Wandhill
32 Kennedy Dr
33 Abelton Gr
34 Orchard Paddock
35 Larch Way
36 Acacia Gr
37 Cyprus Gr
38 Elder Gr
39 Walnut La
40 Minster Cl
B2 1 Farndale Cl
2 Sandholme
3 Newdale
4 Keldale
5 Northcroft
6 Rushwood Cl
7 Lansdown Way
8 Scriven Gr
9 Woodcock Cl
10 Falcon Cl
11 Mallard Way
12 Hall Rise
13 Folks Cl
14 Old Coppice
15 New Forge Ct
16 Chatsworth Dr
17 Riversdale
18 Netherwindings
19 Thornhills
20 Garths End
21 Landings The
22 Landing La
23 Windmill Way
24 Linley Ave
25 West Nooks
C3 1 Langton Ct
2 Woodleigh Cl
3 Oakhill Cres
4 Chaldon Cl
5 Beech Pl
6 Wheatcroft
7 Ryecroft
8 Waincroft
C4 1 Leyfield Cl
2 Moorland Garth
3 Wilkinson Way
4 Fossland View
5 Riverside Wlk
6 Low Croft
7 Wood Cl
8 Adlington Cl
9 Firbank Cl
10 Osmington Gdns
11 Melcombe Ave
12 Portisham Pl
13 Ladysmith Mews
14 Sussex Way
15 Pelham Pl

12
A3 1 Knapton Cl
2 Pasture Cl
3 Whin Cl
4 Cumbrian Ave
5 Humber Dr
6 Cumberland Cl
7 St Wilfrid's Cl
8 St Wilfrid's Rd
9 Old Highway The
A4 1 Orchard Way
2 Middlecroft Gr
3 Glebe Cl
4 Station Sq
5 Highlands Ave
6 Oaklands
7 Hallard Way
8 Willows The
9 West End Cl
10 Oak Tree Way
11 Harvest Cl

16
B2 1 Riverside Wlk
2 Riverside Gdns
3 Bankside Cl
4 Springfield Rd
5 Littlefield Cl
6 Montague Wlk
7 Pear Tree Ave
8 Elm Tree Ave
9 Limegarth
10 Chantry Gap
11 Chantry Gr
12 Grove Gdns
13 Chantry Gr
14 Chantry Ave
15 Apple Garth
16 Cherry Gr
17 Sycamore View
18 Fairway Dr
19 Dikelands Cl
20 Nether Way
21 Riversvale Dr
22 Allerton Dr
23 School La
24 Station Rd
25 Beech Way
26 Beeches The
27 Longridge Gdns
C2 1 Little Garth
2 Hutton Cl
3 Nursery Rd
4 Midway Ave
5 Easthorpe Dr
6 Orchard Rd
7 Linton Rd
8 Sandyridge
9 Long Ridge La

17
C3 1 Chaumont Way
2 Marmiam Dr

19
C2 1 Harolds Way
2 Norseway
3 Hardrada Way
C3 1 Bridlington Rd
2 Derwent Cl
3 Daneswell Cl
4 Burton Fields Rd
5 Garrowby View
6 Kingsway
7 Darley Cl
8 Wharton Rd
9 St John's Rd
10 Church La
11 Egremont Cl
12 Burton Fields Cl
13 Heather Bank
14 Tostig Cl
15 Fairfax
16 School Cl
17 Roman Avenue N
18 Godwinsway
19 Butts Cl
20 Viking Cl
21 Midgley Cl
22 Brown Moor
23 Furlong Rd
24 Etty Cl

25 Stonewall Cottage La

21

C3
1 Bridle Way
2 Hessay Pl
3 Barkston Cl
4 Bramham Gr
5 Branton Pl
6 Barkston Gr

23

A4
1 Stockhill Cl
2 Copper Beeches The
3 Manor Beeches The
4 Manor Dr
5 York St
6 Owlwood La
7 Owlwood Ct
8 Curlew Glebe
9 Copper Beech Cl
B4
1 Gorse Hill
2 Holly Tree Croft
3 Aspen Cl
4 Orchard Cotts
5 Petercroft Cl
6 Kendal Cl
7 Undercroft
8 Thorncroft
9 Sawyers Wlk
10 Coneycroft
11 Keepers Way
12 Westwood Mews
13 Scaudercroft
14 Greencroft Ct
15 Lime Tree Mews
16 Ox Calder Cl
17 Greencroft La
18 Greenside
19 Ashdale Rd
20 Green The
21 Hunters Wood Way
22 Deerstone Way
23 Greenside Wlk
24 Greenside Cl

26

C2
1 Leadley Croft
2 Moorland Gdns
3 Nalton Cl
4 Hobson Cl
5 Homefield Cl
6 Paddock Cl
7 Barnfield Way
8 Wilstrop Farm Rd
9 Manor Farm Cl
10 Westfield Ct
11 Beadle Garth
12 Bellmans Croft
13 Vavasour Ct
14 Deacons Ct
15 St Giles Way
16 Vicars Cl
17 Reygate Gr
18 Malbys Gr
19 Fairfax Croft
20 Church St
21 Sawyer's Cres
C3
1 Larkfield Cl
2 Horseman Cl
3 Lynwood Ave
4 Lynwood View
5 Saddlers Cl
6 Farriers Croft
7 Waggoners Dr
8 Potters Dr
9 Wainers Cl
10 Millers Croft
11 Loriners Dr
12 Gardeners Cl
13 Weavers Pk
14 Coopers Dr
15 Drapers Croft
16 Barbers Dr
17 Hatters Cl
18 Sutor Cl
19 Faber Cl
20 Low Gn
21 Croft Farm Cl
22 Orchard Garth
23 Horseman Ave
24 Horseman Dr

26 Rutland Cl
27 St Nicholas Rd
28 St Nicholas Cres
29 St Nicholas Cl
30 Pike Hills Mount
31 Link The
32 Wheel Wright Cl
33 Thatchers Croft
34 Tadcaster Rd

27

A3
1 Bowyers Cl
2 Wattlers Cl
3 Ropers Ct
4 Ploughman's Cl
5 Learmans Way
6 Whistler Cl
7 Herdsman Dr
8 Fletcher's Croft
9 Ostler's Cl
C1
1 Main St
2 Ferry Farm Cl
3 Maypole Gr
4 St Matthew's Cl
C3
1 Harcourt Cl
2 De Grey Pl
3 Drummond View
4 Beech Ct
5 Vernon Cl
6 Wolsey Dr
7 Melton Dr
8 Neville Dr
9 Lamplugh Cres
10 Garbett Way
11 Keble Cl
12 Keble Dr
13 Keble Park Cres
14 Montague Rd
15 Weavers Cl
16 Orchard The

31

A3
1 White House Gr
2 Beech Cl
3 Lorraine Ave
4 Hillgarth Ct
5 Dovecote Garth
6 Beck Cl
7 Beckside
8 Belvoir Ave
9 Alvin Wlk
B3
1 Riverside Cl
2 Riverside Gdns
3 Church Gn
4 Church La
5 Blacksmiths Cl
6 Jasmine Garth

33

B2
1 Appleton Roebuck Prim Sch
2 Lilac Ave
3 Southfield Grange

34

B4
1 Crescent The
2 Lilac Ave
3 Pleasant Ave
4 Beech Ave
5 Cherry Tree Dr
6 Cundall Dr
7 Willows The
8 Oak Dr
9 Close The
10 Elm Avenue

39

A2
1 Green The
2 Meadows The
3 Orchard View
4 Wheelhouse The
5 Dell The
6 Arthur Pl

41

B4
1 Ploughlands
2 Greenway The
3 Foxcroft
C4
1 Sycamore Cl
2 Furnwood
3 Sunnydale

4 Oak Tree Ct
5 Pinelands
6 Melander Gdns
7 Rosecomb Way
7 Milford Mews
8 Milford Way

42

B2
1 Beaulieu Cl
2 Mendip Cl
3 South Down Rd
4 Grampian Cl
5 Keswick Way
6 White Horse Cl
7 North Moor
8 Northmoor Cl
B3
1 Langley Ct
2 Manor Ct
3 Crinan Ct
4 Trent Ave
B4
1 Northlands Ave
2 Rowley Ct
3 Shilton Garth Cl
4 Firtree Cl

45

A2
1 Coniston Cl
2 Wasdale Cl
3 Garburn Cl
4 Scafell Cl
5 Loweswater Rd
6 Fylingdales Ave
A3
1 Coningham Ave
2 Manor Park Gr
3 Elma Gr
4 Rawcliffe Cl
5 Cheshire Cl
6 Deanhead Gr
7 Swinton Cl
A4
1 Caithness Cl
2 Conway Ct
3 Hatfield Cl
4 Osbourne Dr
5 Greenwich Cl
6 Somerset Cl
7 Highgrove Cl
8 Longwood Link
9 Winscar Gr
10 Broadstone Way
11 Mitchell Way
B2
1 Embleton Dr
2 Coledale Cl
3 Leighton Croft
4 Barmby Cl
5 Grasmere Gr
6 Barden Ct
7 Southolme Dr
8 Milton Carr
9 Fewston Dr
10 Reighton Dr
C1
1 Linden Gr
2 Marten Cl
3 Rainsborough Way
4 Lockyer Cl
C2
1 Caldbeck Cl
2 Stonelands Ct
3 Belmont Cl
4 Hastings Cl
5 Harrow Glade
6 Wimpole Cl
7 Halifax Ct
8 Water La
9 Tamworth Rd
10 Lundy Cl
11 Pentire Cl

46

A2
1 Herdwick Cl
2 Headley Cl
3 Minchin Cl
C4
1 Crabtree Ct
2 Hawthorn Terrace The
3 White Rose Ave
4 Garthway
5 White Rose Gr
6 Conifer Cl

47

A1
1 Kirkham Ave
2 Crossway The
3 Lilling Ave
4 Pinsent Ct
A3
1 Scawton Ave

2 Gormire Ave
3 Rolston Ave
4 Heather Croft
5 Badger Paddock
6 Pinewood Gr
7 Thornfield Dr
B1
1 Albert St
2 Victoria Way
3 Morritt Cl
4 Foston Gr
5 Thornfield Ave
6 Laburnum Garth
B2
1 Dickens Cl
2 Homestead Cl
3 Carrnock Ct
4 Andrew Dr
5 Monkton Rd
6 Theresa Cl
B4
1 Cheviot Cl
2 Cambrian Cl
3 Kendrew Cl
4 Merlin Covert
5 Firwood Whin
6 Oak Glade

49

A1
1 Carnoustie Cl
2 Lochrin Pl
3 Gresley Ct
4 Staithes Cl
A2
1 Sunningdale Cl
2 Troon Ct
3 Greensborough Ave
4 Birkdale Gr
5 Kenrick Pl
6 Muirfield Way
C1
1 Pately Pl
2 Hebdon Rise
3 Baildon Cl
C3
1 Regents Mews
2 Marquis Ct
3 Dukes Ct

50

A1
1 Winchester Gr
2 Garland St
3 Winchester Ave
4 Chatsworth Terr
5 Dilys Gr
6 Peppercorn Cl
7 Bonington Ct
8 Renshaw Gdns
9 Hillary Garth
10 Segrave Wlk
11 Chelwood Wlk
12 Bouthwaite Dr
A2
1 Carrington Ave
2 Yarburgh Gr
3 Oak St
4 Amberly St
5 Linton St
6 Thompson Pl
B2
1 Chudleigh Rd
2 Bromley St
3 Albany St
4 Walworth Street N
5 Hanover Street E
6 Upper Hanover St
7 Hanover Street W
8 Stamford Street W
9 Walworth Street S
10 Stamford Street E
11 Kingsland Terr
12 Brunel Ct
13 St Barnabas Ct
14 Regents Ct
15 Victoria Ct
16 Carlisle St
17 Carleton St
C3
1 Rosslyn St
2 Westerdale Ct
3 Skelton Ct
C4
1 Belcombe Way
2 Hudson Cres
3 Clifton Pl
4 Pinfold Ct

51

A4
1 Glencoe St

2 Back West View
3 Shipton St
B4
1 Upper Newborough St
2 Allan St
3 Murrough Wilson Pl
4 Feversham Cres
5 Hillsborough Terr
6 Hudson St

52

A2
1 Hawthorn St
2 Emmerson St
3 Fleming Ave
4 Scrope Ave
A3
1 Dennison St
2 Villa Gr
C2
1 Melrose Ct
2 Appleby Pl
3 Ingleton Wlk
4 Woodhouse Gr
5 Hornby Ct

53

B1
1 Vicarage Gdns
2 St Thomas's Cl
3 Givendale Gr

54

A1
1 Redcoat Way
2 Kitemere Pl
3 Hawkshead Cl
4 Osprey Cl
5 Pheasant Dr
6 Houndsway
7 Eaton Ct
8 Hatfield Wlk
A2
1 Askham Croft
2 Minter Ct
3 Waterman Ct
4 Salmond Rd
5 Otterwood Bank
6 Beechwood Glade
7 Cedarwood Cl
8 Apple Blossom Ct
9 St Josephs Ct
10 St Michaels Ct
A4
1 Croftside
2 Croftway
3 Hammerton Cl
B1
1 Hinton Ave
2 Lydham Ct
3 Martin Cheeseman Ct
4 Cranfield Pl
B2
1 Thornwood Covert
2 Maplewood Paddock
3 Foxwood La
4 Fir Heath Cl
B4
1 Kirk View
2 Church Mews
3 Elmtree Gdns
4 Oak Rise
5 Cross St
6 Gale Farm Ct
C1
1 Farmlands Rd
2 Dringfield Cl
3 Herdsman Rd
4 Sandcroft Cl
5 Deepdale
C2
1 Woodford Pl
2 Kempton Cl
3 Clay Pl
4 Chesney Fields
5 St James Ct

55

A1
1 Turnmire Rd
2 Southfield Cres
3 Meadow Ct
4 Pastures The
5 St Helen's Rd
B1
1 Kensington Ct
2 Regency Mews
3 Calcaria Ct
B3
1 Harlow Ct
2 Heath Cl
3 Holly Bank Gr
4 Jennifer Gr

5 Mildred Gr
6 Anderson Gr
7 Nigel Gr
8 Trevor Gr
B4
1 Falconer St
2 Barrett Ave
3 Barbara Gr
4 Caroline Cl
5 Robin Gr
C3
1 Towton Ave
2 Trentholme Dr
3 Moorgarth Ave
4 White House Gdns
C4
1 Enfield Cres
2 Watson Terr
3 Cecilia Pl
4 Cambridge St
5 Oxford St
6 Mount Ephraim
7 Holgate Bridge Gdn

56

A2
1 Windsor St
2 Hubert St
3 Ruby St
4 Count De Burgh Terr
5 Balmoral Terr
6 Lichfield Ct
A3
1 Telford Terr
2 Philadelphia Terr
3 Adelaide St
C1
1 Stockholm Cl
2 Danes Croft

57

A1
1 Endfields Rd
2 Crosslands Rd
3 Broadway Gr
A4
1 Brinkworth Terr
2 Thomas St
3 Hilda St
4 Granville Terr
5 Lansdowne Terr
6 Herbert St
7 Chaucer St
8 Daysfoot Ct
9 Apollo St
10 Tannery The
11 Lawrence St
12 Leake St
B1
1 Wilsthorpe Gr
2 Tilmire Cl
3 Low Moor Ave
B4
1 St Nicholas Pl
2 Arnside Pl
C2
5 Goodricke Way
C4
1 Heathfield Rd
2 Owston Ave
3 Waynefleet St
4 Cycle St
5 Norman St

58

A2
1 Enclosure Gdns
2 Heslington Ct
3 Holburns Croft
B4
1 Shallowdale Gr
2 Bracken Hill
3 Kimberlows Wood Hill
4 Pinewood Hill

59

A4
1 Halladale Cl
2 Tarbert Cres
3 Wansbeck
4 Cairnborrow
B4
1 Quaker Gn
2 Lindale
3 Crummock
4 Miterdale
5 Stonethwaite
6 Bannisdale
7 Troutbeck

65

B1
1 Victoria St
2 Drake St
3 Spencer St
4 Clement St